ATTAINING
SALVATION
DEVOUT REFLECTIONS
AND MEDITATIONS

*"As I live, saith the Lord God, I
desire not the death of the wicked,
but that the wicked turn from his
way, and live."* —Ezechiel 33:11

St. Alphonsus Liguori
1696-1787
Bishop and Doctor of the Church

ATTAINING SALVATION

DEVOUT REFLECTIONS AND MEDITATIONS

By

St. Alphonsus Liguori

Translated from the Italian by

Fr. Edmund Vaughan

OF THE CONGREGATION OF THE MOST HOLY REDEEMER

TAN BOOKS AND PUBLISHERS, INC.
Rockford, Illinois 61105

Permissu Superiorum.

Imprimatur   ☩ Herbert Cardinal Vaughan
             Archbishop of Westminster
             March 28, 1901

Originally published by Burns & Oates, Limited, London, in 1901, as *Devout Reflections on Various Spiritual Subjects for the Profit of Souls Who Desire to Advance in Divine Love,* by St. Alphonsus de'Liguori. Retypeset with minor updating (primarily of punctuation) and published in 2008 by TAN Books and Publishers, Inc. as *Attaining Salvation: Devout Reflections and Meditations.*

ISBN 978-0-89555-883-1

Cover Design: Milo Persic

Cover photo: Kreicher/iStockphoto.com

Printed and bound in the United States of America.

TAN BOOKS AND PUBLISHERS, INC.
P.O. Box 424
Rockford, Illinois 61105
1982

"One soul, one eternity!"
—St. Teresa of Avila

Do not be astonished at the difficulties one meets in the way of mental prayer, and the many things to be considered in undertaking this heavenly journey. The road upon which we enter is a royal highway which leads to heaven. Is it strange that the attainment of such a treasure should cost us something? The time will come when we shall realize that the whole world could not purchase it.

—St. Teresa of Avila

Contents

Preface

THIS little work of St. Alphonsus was translated and published, together with a series entitled *Reflections on the Passion of our Lord,* in 1849. The edition is now exhausted, and the work out of print. The *Devout Reflections on Spiritual Subjects* have been re-translated and are here published separately in a convenient form. The *Reflections on the Passion* will also be brought out in the same style.

Both works both composed and published together by the Saint when he was in the seventy-eighth year of his age. He was still governing the Episcopal See of St. Agatha, in the Kingdom of Naples, but he was so broken down in health and so crippled by most painful infirmities that it seemed a miracle that he should still be able not only to watch over the affairs of his diocese but even to apply himself to the composition of several important and learned works.

Referring to these labors, the Saint's learned and pious biographer, Cardinal Villecourt, remarks: "In the midst of all his sufferings of body and mind, St. Alphonsus profited by every moment of leisure to contribute by his writings to the glory of God. Thus in 1773 he published *Reflections on the Passion of Jesus Christ,* and in the same volume a number of *Devout Reflections on Spiritual Subjects.* Everyone saw in this little work a loadstone, as it were, to attract the hearts of men and unite them to that of Jesus Christ."

On the occasion of its first publication in Naples, Canon Simioli was charged by Cardinal Sersale, the Archbishop, with the examination of the work. He gave his opinion of it in these terms: "I cannot express how great is my esteem for this little book, which is so well calculated to stir up piety and banish tepidity and negligence, especially in these unhappy times, in which charity has grown cold and scandals are multiplied. It is to this pious author that we shall owe the consolation of seeing the fire of divine love enkindled in hearts that are cold, and burning with greater ardor in souls that are fervent." St. Alphonsus himself, in a letter written in the same year, 1773, to one of his penitents, says: "I send you two little works, the first of which may assist you in meditating on the Passion of Jesus Christ; I myself make use of it every day. I read likewise, every day, something from the second book, entitled *Devout Reflections*. I should wish you to do the same, for I have composed it especially for those who desire to give themselves entirely to God."

To such recommendations nothing could be added. And we can only hope and pray that this little work, one of the last written by St. Alphonsus, may be as fruitful of grace now, and in this our country, as it was in his native land, when first it came forth from the pen of the holy Doctor.

E. V.

St. Mary's, Clapham
Palm Sunday, 1901

ATTAINING SALVATION

DEVOUT REFLECTIONS
AND MEDITATIONS

"For what doth it profit a man, if he gain the whole world, and suffer the loss of his own soul? Or what exchange shall a man give for his soul?" —Matthew 16:26

Reflection 1

On the Thought of Eternity

SAINT AUGUSTINE used to call the thought of eternity "The Great Thought." This thought made the Saints count all the treasures and grandeurs of this life as nothing more than straw, mire, smoke and dung. This thought has driven so many anchorites [hermits] to hide themselves in deserts and caves, and so many noble youths, and even kings and emperors, to shut themselves up in cloisters. This thought has given courage to so many martyrs to endure racks and iron nails and red-hot gridirons and even being burned alive.

No, we are not created for this earth. The end for which God has placed us in the world is this, that by our good works we may merit eternal life. "The end [is] life everlasting." (*Romans* 6:22). And therefore St. Eucherius used to say that the only affair that we should attend to in this life is eternity, that is, to gain for ourselves a happy eternity and escape a miserable one. "The business for which we work is eternity." If we make sure of success in this business, we shall be happy forever; if we fail in it, we shall be forever miserable.

Happy is he who lives with eternity always in view, with a lively faith that he must shortly die and enter into eternity. "The just man liveth by faith," says the Apostle. (*Galatians* 3:11). It is faith that makes the just live in the grace of God and that gives life to their

1

souls by detaching them from earthly affections and reminding them of the eternal goods which God holds out to those who love Him.

St. Teresa used to say that all sins had their origin in an absence of faith. Therefore, in order to overcome our passions and temptations, we must frequently revive our faith by saying: "I believe in the life everlasting." I believe that after this life, which for me will quickly finish, there is an eternal life, either full of delights or full of torments, which will be my lot according to my merits or demerits.

St. Augustine also was accustomed to say that a man who believes in eternity and yet is not converted to God has lost either his reason or his faith. "O eternity!" these are his words, "he that meditates upon thee and repents not, either has no faith, or if he has faith, he has no heart." In reference to this, St. John Chrysostom relates that the Gentiles, when they saw Christians committing sin, called them either liars or fools. If you believe not (they said) what you say you believe, you are liars; if you believe in eternity and sin, you are fools. "Woe to sinners who enter into an eternity which is to them unknown because they would not reflect upon it," exclaims St. Cæsarius; and then he adds: "But alas, O double woe, they enter it and they never come forth!" Wretched beings! For them the gates of Hell open only to admit them, not to release them.

St. Teresa used to repeat to her spiritual daughters: "My children, one soul, one eternity!" She meant to say: My children, we have but one soul, and if that is lost, all is lost; and once lost, it is lost forever. In a word, upon that last breath which we draw in dying depends our being either happy forever, or forever in despair. If the eternity of the next life—if Paradise, if Hell—were mere opinions of literary men and things of doubtful reality, even then we ought to take every care to live well and not run the risk of losing our soul forever. But no, for these things are not doubtful; they are certainties; they are truths of faith, much more certain than the things which we see with the eyes of the body.

Let us, then, pray to Our Lord to give us more faith, saying with the Apostles: "Lord, increase our faith!" For, if we are not strong in faith, we may become worse than Luther or Calvin. On the contrary, one thought of lively faith in the eternity that awaits us may make us saints.

St. Gregory says that they who meditate on eternity are neither puffed up by prosperity, nor cast down by adversity because, as they desire nothing in the world, so they fear nothing from the world.

When it happens to us to suffer any infirmities or persecutions, let us remember the Hell which we have deserved by our sins. When we do this, every cross will seem to us light, and we shall thank the Lord and say: It is "the mercies of the Lord that we are not consumed." (*Lamentations* 3:22). Let us say with David, "Unless the Lord had been my helper, my soul had almost dwelt in hell." (*Psalms* 93:17). If God had not shown me mercy, I should already have been in Hell, even from the time in which I first offended Him by a grievous sin. Through my own fault I was already lost; it is Thou, O God of mercy, that hast stretched out Thy hand and hast drawn me forth from Hell, "Thou hast delivered my soul, that it should not perish." (*Isaias* 38:17).

O my God, Thou knowest well how often I have deserved Hell; but notwithstanding this, Thou dost command me to hope, and I will hope. My sins terrify me, but Thy death and Thy promise of pardon to him that repents encourage me. "A contrite and humbled

heart, O God, Thou wilt not despise." (*Psalms* 50:19).
I have despised Thee in times past, but now I love
Thee above all things, and I grieve more than for any
other evil that I have offended Thee. O my Jesus, have
pity on me.

Mary, Mother of God, intercede for me.

Reflection 2

We Are Pilgrims on Earth

AS LONG as we are in this life, we are so many pilgrims wandering upon the earth, far from our true country, which is Heaven, where God awaits us, that we may rejoice forever in beholding His beautiful countenance. "While we are in the body," writes the Apostle, "we are absent from the Lord." (*2 Corinthians* 5:6). If then we love God, we ought to have a continual desire to leave this place of exile by being separated from the body, that we may go and behold Him. It was for this that St. Paul ever sighed, as he goes on to say: "We are confident, and have a good will to be absent rather from the body, and to be present with the Lord." (*2 Corinthians* 5:8).

Before the Redemption, the way to God was closed for us miserable sons of Adam; but Jesus Christ, by His death, has obtained for us the grace of having it in our power to become the sons of God. ["But as many as received Him, He gave them power to be made the sons of God." (*John* 1:12)]. And thus He has opened to us the gates by which we can have access, as children, to God our Father.

On this account St. Paul says: "Now, therefore, you are no more strangers and foreigners, but you are fellow-citizens with the Saints and the domestics of God," (*Ephesians* 2:19), so that, while we are in the grace of God, we enjoy the citizenship of Paradise and belong

5

to the household of God. St. Augustine says: "Nature corrupted by sin produces citizens of an earthly city and vessels of wrath; but grace, which frees our nature from sin, makes us citizens of a heavenly country and vessels of mercy."

This made David say: "I am a sojourner on the earth; hide not Thy commandments from me." (*Psalms* 118:19). O Lord, I am a pilgrim upon this earth; teach me to keep Thy precepts, which are the road by which I may reach my country in Heaven. It is not surprising that the wicked should wish to live forever in this world, for they justly fear that they will pass from the pains of this life to the eternal and far more terrible pains of Hell; but how can he who loves God, and has a moral certainty that he is in the state of grace, desire to go on living in this vale of tears—in continual bitterness, in anxieties of conscience, in peril of being condemned? How can he help sighing to depart speedily to unite himself to God in a blessed eternity, where there is no longer any danger of losing Him? Oh how the souls who love God continually, as long as they live, groan and cry out with David: "Woe is me, that my sojourning is prolonged!" (*Psalms* 119:5). Unhappy is he who must continue to live a long time in this world, in the midst of so many perils to his salvation! Therefore it is that the Saints have continually had this prayer upon their lips: "Thy kingdom come"; quickly, O Lord, quickly take us to Thy kingdom. Let us make speed, then, as the Apostle exhorts us, to enter that country where we shall find perfect peace and contentment: "Let us hasten therefore to enter into that rest." (*Hebrews* 4:11). Let us hasten, I say, with desire, and not cease to press onwards, till we are safe in that blessed harbor of rest which God prepares for them that love Him.

He that runs in a race, says St. John Chrysostom, pays no heed to the spectators, but only to the crown of victory; he stops not, but the nearer he approaches the goal, the quicker he runs. Therefore, the Saint concludes that the longer we have lived, the more we should hasten by good works to secure the prize, so that our only prayer for relief in the troubles and trials which we endure in this life ought to be this: "Thy kingdom come." Lord, may Thy kingdom speedily come, where, united eternally to Thee and loving Thee face to face with all our powers, we shall no longer have fear or danger of losing Thee.

And when we find ourselves afflicted by trials or despised by the world, let us comfort ourselves with the great reward which God prepares for those who suffer for the love of Him: "Be glad in that day and rejoice, for behold, your reward is great in heaven." (*Luke* 6:23). St. Cyprian says that with good reason our Lord wills that we should rejoice in labors and persecutions, because then the true soldiers of God are tried and crowns are distributed to those who are faithful.

Behold, O my God, my heart is ready; behold me prepared for every cross which Thou shalt send me. No, I desire not delights or pleasures in this life; he who has offended Thee and deserves Hell merits not pleasures. I am ready to suffer all the infirmities and adversities which Thou dost send me; I am ready to embrace all the contempt of men. I am content, if so it please Thee, to be deprived of all bodily and spiritual consolations; it is enough if Thou dost not deprive me of Thyself and of loving Thee forever. I deserve not this, but I hope for it, through the blood that Thou hast shed for me. I love Thee, O my God, my Love, my All. I shall live forever, and I hope I shall love Thee forever; and my paradise will ever be to rejoice in Thine infinite bliss, for Thou dost truly merit it because of Thine infinite goodness.

God Deserves to Be Loved Above Everything

SAINT TERESA says that it is a great favor that God bestows upon a soul when He calls it to love Him. Let us then love Him, since we are called to this love, and let us love Him as He desires to be loved. "Thou shalt love the Lord thy God with thy whole heart." (*Matthew* 22:37). The Venerable Luis de Puente felt ashamed at saying to God: "O Lord, I love Thee above everything; I love Thee more than all creatures, more than all riches, than all honors, than all earthly pleasures," for it seemed to him that it was like saying: "My God, I love Thee more than straw and smoke and mire."

But God is satisfied when we love Him above all things. Therefore, at least let us say to Him: "Yes, O Lord, I love Thee more than all the honors of the world, more than all its riches, more than all my relations and friends; I love Thee more than health, more than my good name, more than knowledge, more than all my comforts; in a word, I love Thee more than everything I possess—more than myself."

And let us still further say: "O Lord, I value Thy graces and Thy gifts; but more than all Thy gifts, I love Thyself, who alone art Infinite Goodness and a Good infinitely amiable and surpassing every other good. And, therefore, O my God, whatever Thou mayest give me besides Thyself, which is not Thyself, is not sufficient for me; if Thou givest me Thyself, Thou alone art sufficient for me. Let others seek what they will, I will seek nothing but Thee alone, my love, my all. In Thee alone I find all that I can seek or desire."

The sacred Spouse said that among all things, she had chosen to love her beloved: "My beloved is white and ruddy, chosen out of thousands." (*Canticle of Canticles* 5:10). And whom, then, shall we choose to love? Among all our friends of this world, where can we find a friend more worthy of love and more faithful than God; and who has loved us more than God? Let us pray, then, and let us pray constantly: "O Lord, draw me after Thee," for if Thou dost not draw me after Thee, I cannot come to Thee.

O Jesus, my Saviour, when will it be that, stripped of every other affection, I shall desire and seek for nothing but Thee! I would gladly detach myself from everything, but certain importunate affections often enter my heart and draw me away from Thee. Do Thou then, by Thy powerful hand, detach me from them and make Thyself the only object of all my affections and all my thoughts.

St. Augustine says that he who has God has everything, and he who has not God has nothing. What does it profit a rich man to possess many treasures of gold and jewels, if he has not God? What does it profit a monarch to have many kingdoms, if he has not the grace of God? What does it profit a man of letters to understand many sciences and languages, if he knows not how to love his God? What does it profit a general to command an entire army, if he lives the slave of the devil and far from God? When David was already king, but in a state of sin, he walked in his gardens, he went to his sports and to other pleasures, but all creatures seemed to say to him: "Where is thy God? Wouldst thou seek in us thy happiness? Go, find God, whom thou hast left, for He alone can give thee contentment." And therefore David confessed that in the midst of all his pleasures he found no peace and wept night and day, with the thought that he was without God. "My tears have been my bread day and night, whilst it is said to me daily: Where is thy God?" (*Psalms* 41:4).

In the midst of the miseries and troubles of this world, who can console us better than Jesus Christ? Therefore He says to us: "Come to Me, all you that labor and are burdened, and I will refresh you." (*Matthew* 11:28). Oh the folly of worldlings! One single tear shed through sorrow for our sins gives more consolation, one aspiration, "My God!" uttered with love by a soul in the state of grace, is worth more than a thousand festivals, a thousand plays, a thousand banquets, in giving contentment to a heart that loves the world. I say again, Oh, folly—and a folly which will be past remedy—when there comes that death in which it is night, as the Gospel says: "The night cometh, when no man can work." (*John* 9:4). Wherefore, Our Lord warns us to walk while the light favors us; for if the night overtakes us, we shall not be able to do anything. Therefore, let God alone be all our treasure, all our love; and let all our desire be to please God, who will not suffer us to conquer Him in love. He rewards a hundredfold everything that is done to give Him pleasure.

> Then silence, wicked world! depart;
> Seek not esteem or love of mine;
> Another Lover owns my heart;
> His charms are greater far than thine.

O my God, and my only Good, be Thou the ruling power in my soul; and as in love I prefer Thee before all things, so do Thou make me in all things prefer

Thy pleasure to any satisfaction of my own. O my Jesus, I trust in Thy blood, that during the rest of my life I shall love nothing but Thee upon this earth, so that I may come one day to possess Thee forever in the kingdom of the Blessed.

O holy Virgin, succor me with thy powerful prayers, and take me to kiss thy feet in Paradise.

To Become Holy, A Soul Must Give Itself to God without Reserve

SAINT PHILIP NERI used to say that so much of our love as we fix upon creatures we take away from God, and therefore our Saviour, as St. Jerome writes, is jealous of our hearts. As He Himself loves us exceedingly, He desires to reign alone in our hearts and to have no companions there to rob Him of a portion of that love which He wills to have entirely for Himself; hence, it displeases Him to see us attached to any affection which is not for Him. And does our Saviour then demand too much, after having given us all His blood and His life, dying upon a cross? Does He not deserve to be loved by us with all our hearts and without reserve?

St. John of the Cross says that every attachment to creatures hinders us from belonging wholly to God. "Who will give me wings like a dove, and I will fly and be at rest?" said the Psalmist. (*Psalms* 54:7). There are some souls called by God to become saints, but because they come to Him with reserve and do not give Him their whole love, but retain some affection for earthly things, they do not become, and never will become, saints. They gladly would fly to God, but being held down by some attachment, they do not fly, but remain

12

always on earth. We must, therefore, detach ourselves from everything. Every thread, says the same St. John, whether thick or slender, hinders the soul from flying to God.

St. Gertrude one day asked Our Lord to make known to her what He desired of her. Jesus answered: "I desire nothing from thee but a heart that is empty." And it was this which David sought from God: "Create a clean heart in me, O God." (*Psalms* 50:12). O my God, give me a pure heart that is emptied and stripped of every earthly affection.

"All for all," wrote Thomas à Kempis. To gain all, we must give all. To possess God, we must leave all that is not God. Then indeed the soul can say to Him: "My Jesus, I have left all for Thee; now give Thyself all to me." To attain to this state, we must not cease to beg of God that He would fill us with His holy love. Love is that mighty fire which consumes every affection in our hearts that is not for God. St. Francis de Sales used to say that, when a house is in flames, we throw all the furniture out of the windows, by which he meant that when a soul is inflamed and divine love takes possession of it, it has no need of sermons or spiritual directors to detach it from the world; the love of God itself will burn and strip the heart of every impure affection.

Divine love is represented in the Sacred Canticles under the symbol of a wine-cellar: "He brought me into the cellar of wine; he set in order charity in me." (*Canticle of Canticles* 2:4). In this blessed cell, souls which are the spouses of Christ, inebriated with the wine of holy love, lose all relish for the things of the world, see God alone, seek God alone in all things, speak only of God and desire not to hear anything but of God alone; and when they hear others speak of riches, dignities and pleasures, they turn to God and say to Him with a burning sigh: "My God, and my all! My God, what is the world to me? What are pleasures, what are honors to me? Thou art all my treasure, all my contentment." St. Teresa, speaking of the prayer of union, says that this union consists in dying to all worldly objects in order to possess nothing but God.

That a soul may give itself wholly to God, three principal means are to be employed: The first is to flee from all defects, even the least, and also to repress every little inordinate desire, such as curiosity in seeing or hearing, and to refrain from certain little pleasures of sense, from certain witty but useless remarks, and such like; secondly, among things which are good, always to choose that which is the best and the most pleasing to God; and thirdly, to receive from the hands of God, with peace of mind and thanksgiving, the things which are displeasing to our self-love.

O my Jesus, my Love, my All, how can I see Thee dying upon a shameful gibbet, despised by all and consumed with anguish, and yet seek for myself earthly pleasures and glory? I will be wholly Thine. Forget the offenses I have committed against Thee, and receive me. Teach me to know from what things I ought to detach myself and what I must do to please Thee, for I resolve to do all. Give me strength to keep my resolution and to be faithful to Thee. O my beloved Redeemer, Thou dost desire that I should give myself all to Thee without reserve in order to unite myself wholly to Thy heart. Behold, this day I give myself all to Thee, all without reserve, all—all! From Thee I hope for grace to be faithful to Thee till death.

O Mother of God, and my own Mother Mary, obtain for me holy perseverance.

Reflection 5

The Two Great Means for Becoming Holy: Desire and Resolution

ALL holiness consists in loving God. Divine love, says Holy Scripture, "is an infinite treasure to men! which they that use, become the friends of God." (*Wisdom* 7:14). God is ready to give us this treasure of His holy love, but He requires that we should greatly desire it. He that little desires any good thing, takes little trouble to obtain it. On the other hand, St. Lawrence Justinian says that a great desire lightens the labor and gives strength.

And thus, he who has little ambition to advance in divine love, instead of becoming more ardent in the pursuit of perfection, will go on becoming always more lukewarm; and continuing thus tepid, he will be in great peril of falling at last down some precipice [i.e., into some mortal sin]. On the other hand, whoever aspires with fervent desires after perfection, and makes efforts daily to advance, will little by little in time attain it. St. Teresa says: "God does not bestow many favors, except on those who earnestly desire His love." And again: "God leaves no good desire without its reward." Therefore, the Saint exhorted everyone not to suffer his desires to slacken, because, "trusting in God and striving our best, little by little, we shall reach that

15

point which the Saints reached."

It is a deceit of the devil (according to the opinion of the same Saint) which makes some think that it is pride to desire to become saints. It would be pride and presumption if we trusted in our own efforts or resolutions, but not if we hope for all from God. For if we do so, He will give us that strength which we have not. Let us, then, desire with a very great desire to attain to a sublime degree of divine love, and let us say with courage: "I can do all things in Him who strengtheneth me." (*Philippians* 4:13). And if we do not find that we possess this great desire, at least let us seek it urgently from Jesus Christ, for He will give it to us.

We will now pass on to the second means—resolution. Good desires must be accompanied by a determined will to make great efforts for the attainment of the good desired. Many desire perfection, but never take the means to gain it; they wish to go and live in a desert, to do great penances and practice great prayer and endure martyrdom; but all such desires are nothing better than mere fancies, which, instead of benefitting them, do them great harm. These are the desires which "kill the slothful," as the Scripture says. (*Proverbs* 21:25). For, such a person, feeding himself upon these fruitless desires, pays no heed meantime to the correction of his defects, the mortification of his appetites, and patience in suffering contempt and contradictions. He wishes to do great things, but such as are incompatible with his present condition; and thus his imperfections increase. In every adversity he is disturbed, every infirmity makes him impatient; and thus he lives always imperfect, and imperfect he dies.

If then we truly desire to become saints, let us resolve first to avoid every venial sin, however slight; secondly, to detach ourselves from every affection to earthly things; thirdly, let us never omit our accustomed exercises of prayer and mortification, however great may be the weariness and disgust we feel in them; fourthly, let us meditate daily on the Passion of Jesus Christ, which inflames with divine love every heart that meditates upon it; fifthly, let us resign ourselves in peace to the will of God in all things that annoy us. Father Balthasar Alvarez used to say: "He that in troubles resigns himself to the Divine Will runs to God post-haste." And, sixthly, let us continually beg of God the gift of His holy love.

Resolution, resolution! St. Teresa often said: "The devil has no dread of irresolute souls." On the contrary, he who really resolves to give himself to God will overcome even what seemed to him insuperable. A resolute will conquers everything. Let us endeavor to repair lost time. The time that remains, let us give it all to God. All time that is not spent for God is lost. Why do we delay? Is it that God should abandon us in our luke-warmness, which may lead us at last to utter ruin? No, let us take courage, and from this day forth act upon this holy maxim: "We have only to please God and die." Souls thus resolute are made by God to fly in the way of perfection.

He that would belong wholly to God must therefore put into practice these resolutions: first, never to commit even the least venial sin; secondly, to give himself to God without reserve, and therefore to neglect nothing which is pleasing to God, provided he has the approval of his director; thirdly, among all good works, to choose what is most pleasing to God; fourthly, not to wait for the morrow, but whatever can be done today, to do it; fifthly, to pray daily to God for an increase in His love. With love, everything will be done; without love, nothing will be done. To gain all, we must give all. Jesus has given Himself entirely to us, that we may be entirely His.

Oh, miserable being that I am! O God of my soul, so many years have I lived upon earth, and what progress have I made in Thy love? My progress has been in my defects, in my self-love, in my sins. And must I live this kind of life even until death? No! Jesus, my Saviour, help me; I will no longer be so ungrateful to Thee as I have been till now. I am resolved truly to love Thee, and I will leave all to please Thee. Stretch out to me Thy hand, O Jesus, Thou who hast shed all Thy blood that Thou might make me Thine. Yes, such I will be, by Thy grace. Death is near; aid me to free myself from everything which hinders me from belonging wholly to Thee, who hast loved me so much. Do this, by Thy merits; from Thee I hope for it.

And I hope it also from thee, O my Mother Mary. By thy prayers, which are all-powerful with God, obtain for me the grace to belong wholly to Him.

Reflection 6

On the Science of the Saints

THERE are two kinds of knowledge upon earth, one heavenly, the other worldly. The heavenly is that which teaches us to please God and to become great in Heaven. The worldly is that which moves us to please ourselves and to become great in this world. But this worldly knowledge is folly and real madness in the sight of God. "For the wisdom of this world is foolishness with God." (*1 Corinthians* 3:19). It is folly, for such wisdom makes fools of those who cultivate it. It makes them fools and like the brutes, for it teaches them to gratify their sensual appetites like the brute beasts.

St. John Chrysostom writes: "We call him a man who preserves unimpaired the likeness of man," namely, that which distinguishes him from a brute. "What is that likeness? The gift of reason." From this it follows that as we should say of a brute which always acted according to reason, that it behaved like a man, so on the contrary, we ought to say of a man who acts according to his sensual appetites and in opposition to reason, that he behaves like a brute beast.

But even speaking of human and natural knowledge of earthly things, what do men know of them, however much they have studied? What are we but so many blind moles, who besides the truths which we know by faith, know all the rest only by means

19

of our senses, or by conjecture, so that everything is for us uncertain and liable to error? What writer on such subjects, however applauded by many, has escaped the criticism of others? But the evil is that, as St. Paul says, "Knowledge" (that is to say, worldly science) "puffs up," and makes men proud and prone to despise others. (Cf. *1 Corinthians* 8:1). And this is a defect most injurious to the soul, for as St. James says, "God resisteth the proud and giveth grace to the humble." (*James* 4:6).

"Oh that they would be wise and would understand and would provide for their last end!" (*Deuteronomy* 32:29). Oh if men would act by reason and the Divine Law—and thus would learn to provide, not so much for a temporal life, which speedily ends, as for eternity— they would certainly not occupy themselves in the attainment of any other knowledge, except such as aids them in obtaining eternal happiness and avoiding eternal torments!

St. John Chrysostom advises us to go to the tombs of the dead in order to learn the science of salvation. Oh what admirable schools of truth are the sepulchers to make us know the vanity of the world! "Let us go to the tombs; there," said the Saint, "there I see nothing but corruption, bones and worms." Among all these skeletons which I see, I cannot tell which belong to the ignorant and which to the learned; I only see that, with death, all the glories of the world were ended for them. What has remained of a Cicero, a Demosthenes, an Ulpian? "They have slept their sleep, and . . . have found nothing in their hands." (*Psalms* 75:6).

Blessed is he who has received from God the science of the Saints. The science of the Saints is to know how to love God. How many in the world are well-versed in literature, in mathematics, in foreign and ancient languages! But what will all this profit them if they know not how to love God? "Blessed is he," said St. Augustine, "who knows God, even if he knows nothing else." He that knows God and loves Him, though he be ignorant of what others know, is more learned than all the learned who know not how to love God.

"The unlearned arise and seize upon Heaven!" cried out the same Saint. How learned were a St. Francis of Assisi, a St. Pascal, a St. John of God! Ignorant in worldly science, but well-skilled in that which is divine. "Thou hast hidden these things from the wise and prudent, and hast revealed them to little ones." (*Matthew* 11:25). By the wise, we are here to understand the worldly-wise, who labor for the possessions and glories of the world and make little account of eternal goods. And by little ones, we are to understand simple souls (like children), who know little of worldly wisdom, but devote all their care to pleasing God.

Oh, let us not then envy those who know many things; let us only envy those who know how to love Jesus Christ; and let us imitate St. Paul, who desired to know nothing but Jesus Christ, and Him crucified; for he says: "I judged not myself to know anything among you, but Jesus Christ, and Him crucified." (*1 Corinthians* 2:2). Happy are we if we attain to the knowledge of the love which Jesus crucified has borne us and from this book of divine love learn to love Him!

O my True and Perfect Lover, where shall I find one who has loved me as much as Thou hast loved me? In the past I have lost my time in learning many things which have profited my soul nothing; and I have thought little of knowing how to love Thee. I see that my life has been lost. I hear Thee calling me to Thy love; behold me here; I leave all; from this day forth, my one, only thought shall be to please Thee, my Supreme Good. I give myself wholly to Thee; do Thou accept me;

give me help to be faithful to Thee; I resolve to be no longer my own, but all, all Thine.

O Mother of God, do thou also succor me by thy prayers.

Reflection 7

Our Eternal Salvation
Is in Prayer

PRAYER is not only useful to us, but necessary for salvation. Hence it is that God, because He desires that we should all be saved, has enjoined it on us by a precept. "Ask, and it shall be given you." (*Matthew* 7:7). It was an error of Wickliff, condemned by the Council of Constance, to say that prayer was a matter of counsel to us, and not of precept. Jesus Christ says, that men "ought always to pray." (*Luke* 18:1). He does not say it is useful or benefitting, but that men "ought always to pray." Wherefore, the Doctors of the Church justly say that a man cannot be excused from grievous [i.e., mortal] sin who neglects to recommend himself to God at least once in a month and whenever he finds himself assaulted by any strong temptation.

The reason for this necessity of recommending ourselves often to God arises from our inability to do any good work or to have any good thoughts of ourselves. "Without Me you can do nothing," says Jesus Christ. (*John* 15:5). And St. Paul teaches the same: "Not that we are sufficient to think anything of ourselves, as of ourselves." (*2 Corinthians* 3:5). Therefore, St. Philip Neri used to say that he despaired of himself. On the other hand, St. Augustine writes that God desires to give us His graces, but does not bestow them, except on those

23

who ask for them. And especially, says the Saint, He only gives the grace of perseverance to those who seek it.

And as the devil never ceases to go about in order to devour us, we ought necessarily to defend ourselves unceasingly by prayer. "Continual prayer is necessary for man," says St. Thomas. And Jesus Christ Himself was the first to teach us: "We ought always to pray and not to faint." (*Luke* 18:1). Otherwise, how shall we be able to resist the incessant temptations of the world and the devil? It was an error of Jansenius, condemned by the Church, to say that the observance of certain precepts was impossible to us and that sometimes the grace which would render it possible is wanting to us. But "God is faithful, who will not suffer you to be tempted above that which you are able," as St. Paul assures us. (*1 Corinthians* 10:13). Yet He requires that when we *are* tempted, we should have recourse to Him for help to resist. St. Augustine writes: "The law is given that grace may be sought; grace is given that the law may be fulfilled." Seeing that the law cannot be obeyed by us without grace, God has yet given us the law in order that we may seek the grace to fulfill it. And this was well expressed by the Council of Trent in these words: "God does not command impossibilities, but in commanding, He admonishes thee both to do what thou canst, and seek aid for what thou canst not do, and He helps thee, that thou mayest be able to do it." (Council of Trent, Session 6, Chapter 11).

Thus, God is very ready to give us His help in order that we may not be overcome by temptation, but this help He gives to those only who have recourse to Him in the time of temptation, and especially in temptations against chastity. For as the Wise Man wrote: "As I knew that I could not otherwise be continent except God gave it . . . I went to the Lord and besought Him." (*Wisdom* 8:21). Let us rest assured that we would not have strength to overcome our carnal appetites if God did not give us help to do so, and this help we shall not have without prayer; but if we pray, we shall assuredly have it in order to resist all the devils of Hell by the power of God, who strengthens us. As St. Paul says: "I can do all things in Him who strengtheneth me." (*Philippians* 4:13).

It also helps us very much to obtain divine grace if we have recourse to the intercession of the Saints, for they have great power with God, especially for the benefit of those who are their special clients. And this is not a mere optional devotion, but is a duty, as St. Thomas writes. For he says that the order established by God requires, that we mortals should receive the helps which are necessary for our salvation through the prayers of the Saints.

With greater force must this apply to the intercession of the Most Holy Virgin Mary, whose prayers are of greater efficacy than those of all the Saints, the more so because, as St. Bernard says, it is through Mary that we have access to Jesus Christ, our Mediator and Saviour. "Through thee," says the holy Doctor, "we have access to the Son, O thou finder of grace, mother of salvation, that through thee He may receive us, who through thee was given to us."*

Let us then pray, and pray with confidence, says the Apostle. "Let us go therefore with confidence to the throne of grace, that we may obtain mercy and find grace in seasonable aid." (*Hebrews* 4:16). Jesus Christ

---

* St. Alphonsus adds here: I think I have sufficiently proved, both in my book called *The Glories of Mary* (Ch. V. § 1, 2) and also in my work *On Prayer* (Ch. 1) the opinion held by many Saints, especially St. Bernard—and by many theologians, as for example, F. Natalis Alexander and F. Contensonius—that all the graces which we receive from God are received by means of Mary. Hence also, St. Bernard says: "Let us seek grace, and let us seek it through Mary; for he that seeks, finds, and cannot be disappointed." The same was said by St. Peter Damian, St. Bonaventure, St. Bernardine, St. Antoninus and others.

now sits on the throne of grace, to console all who have recourse to Him, and says: "Ask, and it shall be given to you." (*Matthew* 7:7). On the day of Judgment also, He will be seated on a throne, but it will be a throne of Justice. What madness, then, will not be theirs who, having it in their power to be relieved of their miseries by going to Jesus now that He sits on a throne of grace, yet wait till He will be their Judge and will no more show mercy. Now He says to us that whatever we ask of Him, if we have confidence, shall all be given to us. "All things whatsoever you ask when you pray, believe that you shall receive, and they shall come to you." (*Mark* 11:24).

And what more can one friend do to another to show his love than to say, "Ask me for what you wish, and I will give it to you?" St. James, moreover, says: "If any of you want wisdom, let him ask of God, who giveth to all men abundantly, and upbraideth not; and it shall be given [to] him." (*James* 1:5). By "wisdom" is here meant the knowledge how to save one's soul; to have this wisdom, we must therefore seek of God the graces necessary to obtain salvation. And will God give them? Assuredly He will give them, and He will give them superabundantly, and more than we ask for. Let us observe also the words, He "upbraideth not." (*James* 1:5). If the sinner repents of his sins and asks salvation from God, God will not act as men do, who reproach the ungrateful with their ingratitude and refuse them what they ask; but He gives to them willingly, as much as and even more than He is asked for. If then we would be saved, we must, even till death, have our lips ever opened to pray and say: "My God, help me; my God, have mercy; Mary, have mercy." If we cease to pray, we shall be lost. Let us pray for ourselves and let us pray for sinners, for this is so pleasing to God. Let us pray also every day for the Holy Souls in Purgatory; those holy prisoners are most grateful to all who pray for them. Moreover, whenever we pray, let us seek graces from God through the merits of Jesus Christ, for He Himself assures us that whatever we ask in His Name, He will give it all to us.

O my God, this is the grace which, above all others, this day I ask of Thee, through the merits of Jesus Christ: grant that throughout my life, and especially in time of temptation, I may recommend myself to Thee and hope for Thy help, for the love of Jesus and Mary.

O holy Virgin, obtain for me this grace, on which depends my salvation.

Reflection 8

I Must One Day Die

IT IS a practice very profitable for our eternal salvation to say often to ourselves: "I must one day die." The Church every year, on Ash Wednesday, gives this reminder to the faithful: "Remember, Man, that thou art dust, and into dust thou shalt return." (Cf. *Genesis* 3:19). And this certainty of death is brought to our recollection very often during the year, sometimes by the burial-grounds which we pass upon the road, sometimes by the tombs which we see in churches, sometimes by the dead who are carried to burial.

The most precious furniture which was carried by the anchorites to their caves was a cross and a skull to remind them of the day of their own death. And thus they persevered in penitential works till the end of their days, and dying in poverty in the deserts, they died more happy than kings who die in their palaces.

"The end is come, the end is come!" cries the Prophet Ezechiel. (*Ezechiel* 7:2). In this world, one man lives a longer, another a shorter time; but for everyone, sooner or later, the end must come; and when that end has come, nothing else will comfort us at the point of death but to have loved Jesus Christ and to have endured with patience the trials of this life for the love of Him. No, at that moment, neither the riches we have acquired, nor the honors we have gained, nor the pleasures we have enjoyed will console us. All the greatness of this world cannot comfort a dying man; it only afflicts him; and the more he has gained of it, the more does he suffer. Sister Margaret of St. Anne, a barefooted Carmelite and daughter of the Emperor Rudolph II, used to say: "What benefit are kingdoms at the hour of death?"

Alas, to how many men of the world does it not happen that, at the very time when they are most engrossed in securing riches, land and honors, they receive the summons of death and have to hear the warning: "Take order with thy house, for thou shalt die, and not live!" (*Isaias* 38:1). "Friend, it is time you should think of making your will, for you are very sick." O God! how great will be the anguish of a man who is about to gain some lawsuit, or come into possession of a mansion or an estate when he hears the priest who has come to recommend his soul to God address to him the words: "Go forth, Christian soul, from this world. Depart from this world, and go to render thy account to Jesus Christ." "But now," he cries, "I am not well prepared." "What matter? Thou must now depart."

O my God, give me light, give me strength, to spend the rest of my life in serving and loving Thee. If now I should have to die, I should not die happy, I should die disturbed. What then do I wait for? Do I wait for death to seize me unprepared, with great danger to my eternal salvation? O Lord, if I have been foolish in the past, I will not be foolish any longer. Now I give myself wholly to Thee; do Thou receive me and help me with Thy grace.

In a word, to everyone that end must come, and with the end will come that moment decisive of a happy or a wretched eternity. O moment on which eternity depends! Oh, that all would think upon that great moment and on the account of their whole life which

they must give at that moment to their Judge! "Oh
that they would be wise and would understand and
would provide for their last end!" (*Deuteronomy* 32:29).
They certainly would not then devote themselves to
amassing riches, or labor to become great in this life,
which must end; but they would think how to become
Saints and to be great in that life which never ends.

If then we have faith, let us believe that there is a
death, a Judgment, an eternity and endeavor, during
the days that yet remain for us, to live only for God.
And therefore let us take care to live as pilgrims on
this earth, remembering that we must speedily leave
it. Let us live with death ever before our eyes, and in
all the affairs of this present life, let us take care to
act as we should act at the point of death. All things
upon earth either leave us, or we have to leave them.
Let us listen to Jesus Christ, who says: "Lay up to
yourselves treasures in heaven, where neither the rust
nor moth doth consume." (*Matthew* 6:20). Let us despise
the treasures of earth, which cannot satisfy us and
which speedily end; and let us gain for ourselves the
treasures of Heaven, which will make us happy and
will never end.

Miserable am I, O Lord, in that I have so often, for
the sake of the goods of earth, turned my back upon
Thee, who art the Infinite Good! I see my folly in having in the past sought to acquire a great name and
make my fortune in the world. From this day forward,
my only ambition shall be to love Thee and in everything to fulfill Thy will. O my Jesus, do Thou take from
me the desire to be seen; make me love contempt and
a hidden life. Give me strength to deny myself in everything which displeases Thee. Make me embrace with
peace, infirmities, persecutions, desolation and all the
crosses Thou shalt send me. Oh, that I could die for

the love of Thee, abandoned by all, as Thou didst die for me!

Holy Virgin, thy prayers can enable me to find my true happiness, which is to love earnestly thy Son. Oh, pray to Him for me; in thee I trust.

Reflection 9

Preparation for Death

DEATH is certain: "It is appointed unto men once to die." (*Hebrews* 9:27). On the contrary, the time and manner of our death is uncertain. Therefore, Jesus Christ exhorts us: "Be you then also ready, for at what hour you think not, the Son of man will come." (*Luke* 12:40). He says: "Be you ready." Therefore, to save our souls, it is not sufficient to prepare ourselves to die when death comes, but we must then be already prepared to embrace it in whatever manner and with whatever circumstances it may come to us. It is accordingly useful for everyone to repeat, at least once a month, the following acts.

Behold me, O my God, ready to embrace that death which Thou dost destine for me. From this moment I accept it, and I sacrifice to Thee my life in honor of Thy Divine Majesty, and also in penance for my sins, rejoicing that this my flesh, to please which I have offended Thee so much, should be devoured by worms and be reduced to dust. O my Jesus I unite the pains and the agony which I must then suffer to the pains and agony which Thou, my Saviour, didst suffer in Thy death. I accept death with all the circumstances Thou mayest appoint; I accept the time, whether it be after many years, or in a short time; I accept the manner, whether in bed or out of it, whether with warning or suddenly,

32

and from that sickness, more or less painful, as it may please Thee. In everything I resign myself to Thy holy Will. Give me strength to suffer all with patience.

"What shall I render to the Lord for all the things that He hath rendered to me?" (*Psalms* 115:12). I thank Thee, O my God, first, for the gift of faith, protesting that I intend to die a child of the Holy Catholic Church. I thank Thee for not having caused me to die when I was in sin, and for having so often pardoned me, with so much mercy. I thank Thee for so many lights and graces with which Thou hast sought to draw me to Thy love. I pray Thee to let me die after receiving Thee in the holy Viaticum, so that, united to Thee, I may go to present myself at Thy tribunal. I do not deserve to hear from Thy mouth the words: "Well done, good and faithful servant: because thou hast been faithful over a few things, I will place thee over many things; enter thou into the joy of thy Lord." (*Matthew* 25:21). I do not deserve it, for in nothing have I been perfectly faithful to Thee; but Thy death gives me hope that I shall be admitted to Heaven, to love Thee there eternally and with all my powers.

O my crucified Love, have mercy upon me! Look upon me with that love with which Thou didst look upon me from the Cross when dying for me. "The sins of my youth and my ignorances do not remember." (*Psalms* 24:7) My sins terrify me, but I am comforted by that Cross on which I see Thee dead for the love of me. "Behold the wood of the cross, on which hung the salvation of the world." (From the Good Friday traditional liturgy). I desire to end my life, that I may cease from offending Thee. Oh, by the blood that was shed for me, do Thou pardon me all my sins before death comes upon me. O blood of the Innocent One, wash away the stains of the guilty!

My Jesus, I embrace Thy Cross and kiss the wounds of Thy sacred feet, before which I desire to breathe out my soul. Ah, do not abandon me at the last moment. "We beseech Thee therefore, save Thy servants, whom Thou hast redeemed with Thy precious blood." I love Thee with all my heart, I love Thee more than myself, and I repent with all my soul that I have despised Thee in the past. O Lord, I was lost, but Thou in Thy goodness hast delivered me from the world; receive then my soul from this moment, for the hour when it shall leave the earth. Therefore, I pray to Thee with St. Agatha: "O Lord, Thou who hast taken from me the love of this world, receive my soul." "In Thee, O Lord, have I hoped; I shall not be confounded forever. . . . Thou hast redeemed me, O Lord, the God of Truth." (*Psalms* 30:1, 6).*

O holy Virgin, succor me at the moment of my death. Holy Mary, Mother of God, pray for me, a sinner, now and at the hour of my death. In thee, O Lady, have I hoped; I shall not be confounded forever. St. Joseph, my protector, obtain for me a holy death. My Guardian Angel, St. Michael the Archangel, defend me in that last conflict with Hell. My holy patrons and all ye Saints of Paradise, succor me in that last moment.

Jesus, Mary and Joseph, be with me at the hour of my death. Amen.

---

* *Psalms* 30:1 has two versions in the Latin Vulgate.

Reflection 10

He that Loves God Must Love and Not Abhor Death

HOW can he ever abhor death who is in the grace of God? "He that abideth in charity abideth in God, and God in him." (*1 John* 4:16). He, therefore, that loves God is secure of His grace, and dying thus, he is sure of going to enjoy Him forever in the kingdom of the Blessed. And shall such a one fear death? David well said: "Enter not into judgment with Thy servant, for in Thy sight no man living shall be justified." (*Psalms* 142:2). This means that no man may presume to be saved by his own merits, for no one but Jesus and Mary can say that he has been without sin throughout his whole life. But he ought not to fear death if, with true repentance for his sins, he trusts in the merits of Jesus Christ, who came on earth to save sinners. "The Son of Man is come to save that which was lost." (*Matthew* 18:11). And in fact He died and poured forth all His blood to save sinners. The blood of Jesus Christ, says the Apostle, speaks more in favor of sinners than the blood of Abel spoke against Cain, who murdered him.

It is true that, without a divine revelation, no man can possess an infallible certainty of his own salvation; but he that has given himself with a sincere heart to God and is ready to lose everything, even life itself, rather than lose the divine grace, has a moral cer-

tainty that he will be saved. The certainty is founded
on the divine promises. "No one," says the Scripture,
"hath hoped in the Lord and hath been confounded."
(*Ecclesiasticus* 2:11). Almighty God declares in so many
passages, that He does not desire the death of the sinner, but that he be converted and saved. "Is it My Will
that a sinner should die, saith the Lord God, and not
that he should be converted from his ways and live?"
(*Ezechiel* 18:23). In another place, He makes the same
declaration, and adds an oath: "As I live, saith the Lord
God, I desire not the death of the wicked, but that the
wicked turn from his way and live." (*Ezechiel* 33:11).
And in the same chapter, God laments over those obstinate sinners who choose to perish because they will
not leave their sins, and says: "Why will you die, O
House of Israel?" (*Ezechiel* 33:11). And to those who
repent of the evil done, He promises to forget all their
transgressions. "If the wicked do penance for all his
sins which he hath committed . . . living, he shall live
and shall not die. I will not remember all his iniquities that he hath done." (*Ezechiel* 18:21-22).

Moreover, when a sinner hates the sin he has committed, it is a certain sign that he has been already
pardoned. A holy Father says that whoever can truly
say with David, "I have hated and abhorred iniquity,"
(*Psalms* 118:163), may be certain of having been for-
given. Another certain sign of having recovered grace
is to have persevered in a good life for a long time after
having sinned. It is also a great sign of being in the
state of grace to have a firm resolution to lose one's life
rather than lose the friendship of God; as also to have
an earnest desire to love Him and to see Him loved by
others, and to feel distress at seeing Him offended.

How is it, then, that certain great Saints, after having given themselves wholly to God, and after a life of
mortification and detachment from all earthly goods,

have felt at the hour of death great terrors at the thought of appearing before Christ their Judge? I reply that those Saints who have suffered these fears at the moment of death have been very few and that it was the Will of God that they should thus purge away some remains of their sins before entering into a blessed eternity, but that, ordinarily speaking, all the Saints have died in great peace and with an ardent desire to die in order to go and see God. And for the rest, there is this difference between sinners and Saints at the hour of death: that sinners from fear pass to despair, and Saints from fear pass to confidence, and thus die in peace.

Therefore, everyone who has signs that he is in the grace of God ought to desire death, repeating the prayer which Jesus Christ has taught us, "Thy kingdom come," and he ought to embrace death with joy when it comes, both in order that he may be freed from sin by leaving this world, where no one lives without imperfections, and that he may go to behold God face to face and love Him with all his strength in the Kingdom of Love.

O my beloved Jesus and my Judge, when Thou shalt judge me, for Thy mercy's sake, condemn me not to Hell. In Hell I could not love Thee, but should have to hate Thee forever; and how could I hate Thee who art so worthy of love and who hast so loved me? If Thou wilt send me to Hell, at least grant me grace to be able to love Thee there with all my heart. On account of my sins, I do not deserve this grace, but if I do not deserve it, Thou hast merited it for me with the blood which Thou didst shed in such agony for me upon the Cross. O my Judge, inflict on me every pain, but deprive me not of the power of loving Thee.

O Mother of God, behold the peril in which I stand of being condemned to be unable to love thy Son, who deserves an infinite love; help me; have pity on me!

Reflection 11

Our Salvation Is in the Cross

"**B**EHOLD the wood of the Cross, on which hung the Salvation of the world!" So sings Holy Church on Good Friday [in her Sacred Liturgy]. In the Cross is our salvation, our strength against temptations, our detachment from earthly pleasures; in the Cross is found true love of God. We must, therefore, resolve to bear with patience that cross which Jesus Christ sends us, and to die upon it for the love of Him, as He died upon His Cross for the love of us. There is no other way to enter Heaven but by resigning ourselves to tribulations until death. And this is the means to find peace, even in suffering. When the cross comes, what means is there, I ask, for not losing peace, except uniting ourselves to the divine will? If we do not take this means, go where we will, do what we may, we shall never escape from the weight of the cross. On the contrary, if we carry it with good will, it will bear us to Heaven and give us peace on earth.

What does he do who refuses the Cross? He increases its weight. But he who embraces it and bears it with patience, lightens its weight, and the weight itself becomes a consolation; for God abounds with graces for all those who carry the cross with a good will in order to please Him. Naturally, there is no pleasure in suffering; but divine love, when it reigns in a heart, makes it take delight in sufferings.

Oh, if only we would consider the state of happiness which we shall enjoy in Paradise if we are faithful to God in enduring trials without complaining! We should not murmur against God, who commands us to suffer, but we should say with Job: "And that this may be my comfort, that afflicting me with sorrow, He spare not, nor I contradict the words of the Holy One." (*Job* 6:10). And if we are sinners and have deserved Hell, this should be our comfort in the tribulations which befall us, to see that we are chastised in this life, because this is the sure sign that God wishes to deliver us from eternal chastisement. Unfortunate is that sinner who prospers in this world! Whoever suffers any grievous trial, let him cast a glance at the Hell which he has deserved, and thus every pain he endures will seem light. If, then, we have committed sins, this ought to be our continual prayer to God: O Lord, spare not pains, but give me, I pray Thee, strength to endure them with patience, that I may not oppose myself to Thy holy Will, "nor I contradict the words of the Holy One," (*Job* 6:10), but in everything conform myself with whatever Thou shalt appoint for me, saying always with Jesus Christ, "Yea, Father, for so hath it seemed good in Thy sight." (*Matthew* 11:26).

The soul which is governed by divine love seeks only God. "If a man should give all the substance of his house for love, he shall despise it as nothing," says Holy Scripture. (*Canticle of Canticles* 8:7). He that loves God despises everything and renounces everything which does not help him to love God; and in all the good works which he does, in his penitential acts and his labors for the glory of God, he does not go seeking his consolations and spiritual sweetness; it is enough for him to know that he pleases God. In a word, he is attentive, ever and in all things, to deny himself, renouncing every pleasure of his own; and having done so, he boasts of nothing and is puffed up with nothing, but calls himself an unprofitable servant, and setting himself in the lowest place, he abandons himself to the divine will and mercy.

We must change our tastes in order to become saints. If we do not arrive at a state in which bitter appears sweet and sweet bitter, we shall never attain to a perfect union with God. In this consists all our security and perfection, in enduring with resignation all things that are contrary to our inclinations, as they happen to us, day by day, whether they are small or great. And we must suffer them for those wise ends for which the Lord desires that we should endure them: first, to purify ourselves from the sins we have committed; secondly, to merit eternal life; thirdly, to give pleasure to God, which is the chief and most noble end which we can aim at in all our actions.

Let us then always offer ourselves to God, to suffer every cross which He may send us; and let us take care to be ever ready to endure every hardship for the love of Him, in order that, when it comes, we may be ready to embrace it, saying, as Jesus Christ said to St. Peter when He was taken in the garden by the Jews to be led to death: "The chalice which My Father hath given Me, shall I not drink it?" (*John* 18:11). God has given me this cross for my good, and shall I say to Him that I will not accept it?

And whenever the weight of any cross seems very great, let us immediately have recourse to prayer, and God will give us strength to carry it meritoriously. And let us then recollect what St. Paul says, that: "The sufferings of this time are not worthy to be compared with the glory to come, that shall be revealed in us." (*Romans* 8:18). Let us, therefore, reanimate our faith whenever tribulations afflict us. Let us first cast a glance upon our crucified Lord, who suffered agonies upon the Cross for our love; and let us then cast a glance up to Paradise, and on the good things which God prepares for those who suffer for His love. And thus we shall not complain, but thank Him for the pains He gives us to endure and ask Him to give us more to suffer. Oh, how the Saints rejoice in Heaven, not that they have possessed honors and pleasures upon earth, but that they have suffered for Jesus Christ! Everything that passes away is trifling; that only is great which is eternal and never passes away.

O my Jesus, how consoling is that which Thou sayest to me: "Turn ye to Me . . . and I will turn to you." (*Zacharias* 1:3). For the sake of creatures and of my own miserable pleasures, I have left Thee; now I leave all and return to Thee; and I am confident that Thou wilt not reject me, if I desire to love Thee, for Thou hast told me that Thou art ready to embrace me, saying: "I will turn to you." Receive me, then, into Thy grace; make me know the great Good which Thou art and the love which Thou hast borne to me, so that I may no more leave Thee. O my Jesus, pardon me; my Beloved, pardon me; my Love, pardon me all the displeasures I have caused Thee. Give me the love of Thee, and then do with me what Thou wilt. Chastise me as much as Thou wilt; deprive me of everything, but deprive me not of Thyself. Let the whole world come and offer me all its goods; I protest that I desire Thee alone and nothing more.

O my Mother, recommend me to thy Son; He gives thee whatever thou askest; in thee I trust.

Reflection 12

How Much It Pleases Jesus Christ that We Suffer for the Love of Him

"**I**F ANY MAN will come after me, let him deny himself, and take up his cross daily, and follow me." (*Luke* 9:23). It will be useful here to make some reflections on these words of Jesus Christ. He says: "If any man will come after me." He does not say: "to me," but "after me." Our Lord desires that we should come after Him; we must therefore walk on the same road of thorns and sufferings in which He walked. He goes before, and does not stop until He reaches Calvary, where He dies. Therefore, if we love Him, we must follow Him, even till death. And thus it is necessary that every one of us should deny himself; that is, that he should deprive himself of everything which self-love demands, but is not pleasing to Jesus Christ.

Our Lord says further: "Let him . . . take up his cross daily, and follow Me." (*Luke* 9:23). Let us consider these last words, one by one. "Let him take up;" it avails little to carry the cross by compulsion; all sinners bear it, but without merit; to bear it with merit, we must embrace it willingly. "His cross"—under this word is implied every kind of tribulation, which is called a "cross" by Jesus Christ, in order that this name may render it sweet, from the thought that He died on a cross for love of us.

He says, moreover, "*his* cross." Some persons, when they receive some spiritual consolation, offer themselves to suffer as much as was endured by the martyrs— racks, nails and red-hot iron plates; but then they cannot endure a headache, the neglect of a friend, the ill temper of a relation. My brother, my sister, God does not ask you to endure racks, nor hot irons, nor piercing nails; but He desires that you should suffer patiently this pain, this contempt, this annoyance. A certain nun would willingly go to suffer in a desert; she would perform great acts of penance; but yet she cannot endure such a one for her superior, or such a one for her companion in her office; but God desires that she should bear that cross which He gives her to suffer, and not that which she would herself choose.

He says "daily." Some persons embrace the cross at first when it comes; but when it lasts long, they say, "Now I can bear it no more." Yet God wills that you should go on enduring it with patience, even if you should have to bear it continually till death. Behold, then, wherein salvation and perfection consist. It is in these few words: "Deny thyself." We must deny our self-love in whatever is wrong. "Take up thy cross," that is, we must embrace the cross which God sends us. "And follow Me": we must follow the footsteps of Jesus Christ, even till death.

We must be persuaded that for this end God keeps us in the world, that we may bear the crosses He sends us, and in this consists the merit of our life. Therefore, our Saviour, because He loves us, came into this world, not for enjoyment, but to suffer, in order that we might follow in His steps. "For unto this are you called, because Christ also suffered for us, leaving you an example, that you should follow His steps." (*1 Peter* 2:21). Let us look at Him, as He goes before with His cross, to trace for us the road by which we must follow Him if we would be saved. Oh what a remedy it is for every trouble that befalls us to say to Jesus Christ: "Lord, is it Thy will that I should endure this cross? I accept it, and will endure it as long as it pleases Thee!"

Many persons are delighted to hear others speak of prayer, of peace, of love for Jesus Christ; but they find little pleasure in hearing anyone speak of crosses and of sufferings. Such persons love Him only so long as they enjoy spiritual sweetness, but if this ceases and there comes some adversity or desolation, in which God hides Himself in order to try them, and deprives them of their accustomed consolations, they leave off prayer, Communions and mortifications and abandon themselves to sadness and lukewarmness and seek comfort in worldly amusements. But these souls love themselves more than Jesus Christ; on the contrary, they who do not love Him with an interested love for the sake of consolations, but with a pure love, and solely because He is worthy of love, do not leave their usual devout exercises for any dryness or weariness which they experience, being content with pleasing God; and they offer themselves to suffer any desolation, even till death and through all eternity, if God should so will it. Jesus Christ, says St. Francis de Sales, is as worthy of love in desolation as in consolation. Souls enamored of God can find their comfort and sweetness in suffering, in recollecting that they suffer for His love, and they say: "How sweet it is, O my Lord, to those who love Thee to suffer for Thee! Oh, that I might die for the love of Thee, my Jesus, who hast died for me!" All this and still more is deserved from us by Jesus Christ, who chose a life of sufferings and a death of pain—without the slightest relief—for love of us, in order to teach us that, if we want to love Him, we must love Him as He loved us. Oh how dear to Jesus

Christ is a soul which suffers and loves Him! O divine gift, gift above every other gift, to love in suffering, and to suffer in loving!

O my Jesus, Thou alone hast been able to teach us these maxims of salvation, all contrary to the maxims of the world; and Thou alone canst give us strength to suffer crosses with patience. I do not pray Thee to exempt me from suffering; I only ask Thee to give me strength to suffer with patience and resignation. O Eternal Father, Thy Son has promised that whatever we ask Thee in His name, Thou wilt give it to us. Behold, we ask this of Thee: give us grace to endure with patience the pains of this life; hear us for the love of Jesus Christ. And Thou, O my Jesus, pardon me all the offenses I have committed against Thee by not being willing to have patience in the trials Thou hast sent me. Give me Thy love, for that will give me strength to suffer all for love of Thee. Deprive me of everything, of every earthly good, of relations, friends, health of body, of every consolation; deprive me even of life, but not of Thy love. Give me Thyself, and I ask Thee no more.

O most holy Virgin, obtain for me love for Jesus Christ, constant, even till death.

Reflection 13

Divine Love Conquers All

"LOVE is strong as death," says the Holy Scripture. (*Canticle of Canticles* 8:6). As death separates us from all the goods of earth, from riches, from honors, from relations, from friends and from all worldly pleasures, so the love of God, when it reigns in a heart, strips it of all affection for these perishable goods. Therefore, the Saints have been seen to strip themselves of everything the world offered them, renounce their possessions, the highest dignities and all they had and fly into deserts or cloisters, to think only on loving God.

The soul cannot exist without loving either the Creator or creatures. Find a soul detached from every earthly love, and you will find it all filled with divine love. Would we know whether we have given ourselves wholly to God? Let us examine ourselves, whether we are weaned from every earthly thing.

Some persons lament that in all their devotions, prayers, Communions, visits to the Blessed Sacrament, they do not find God. To such, St. Teresa says: "Detach your heart from creatures, then seek God, and you will find Him." You will not always find spiritual sweetness, which God does not give without interruption in this life to those who love Him, but only from time to time, to excite in them a longing for those boundless delights which He prepares for them in Paradise; but yet He lets them taste that inward peace which excels all sensual delights, that "peace of God, which," says the Apostle, "surpasseth all understanding." (*Philippians* 4:7). And what greater delight can be enjoyed by a soul which ardently loves God than to be able to say with true affection: "My God and my all"? St. Francis of Assisi continued a whole night in an ecstasy of Paradise, continually repeating these words: "My God and my all."

"Love is as strong as death." (*Canticle of Canticles* 8:6). If a dying man were seen moving towards anything, he would give a sign that he was not dead. Death deprives us of everything. He that would give himself altogether to God must leave everything. If he reserves anything, he gives a sign that his love for God is not perfect, but weak.

Divine love strips us of everything. Father Segneri, an eminent servant of God, used to say: "Love for God is a beloved thief, who robs us of every earthly thing." Another servant of God, when he had given to the poor all his possessions and was asked what had reduced him to such poverty, took the book of the Gospels out of his pocket and said: "See, this is what has robbed me of everything." In a word, Jesus Christ will possess our whole heart, and He will have no companion there. St. Augustine writes, that the Roman Senate refused to allow adoration to be paid to Jesus Christ because He was a proud God, who claimed to be honored alone. And so it is, for as He alone is Our Lord, He has every right to be adored and loved by us with an individual love.

St. Francis de Sales says that the pure love of God consumes everything which is not of God. When, therefore, there arises in our heart any affection for something which is not of God, or not loved for the sake of

God, we must instantly banish it, saying: "Depart, there is no room here for thee." In this consists that complete renunciation which Our Lord so much recommends, if we would be wholly His; it must be total, that is, of everything, and especially of our relations and friends. How many, by trying to please men, have failed to become saints! David has said: "They . . . that please men . . . have been confounded, because God hath despised them." (*Psalm* 52:6).

But above all, we must renounce ourselves, by conquering self-love—cursed self-love, which wants to introduce itself into everything, even our holiest actions, by placing before us our own glory or our own pleasure! How many preachers, how many writers, thus lose all their labors! Frequently, even in prayer, in spiritual reading, or in Holy Communion, there enters some motive which is not pure, either the desire of being noticed, or of enjoying spiritual consolations. We must, therefore, be attentive to beat down this enemy who makes us lose our best actions. Hence, we must deprive ourselves, as far as possible, of whatever most pleases us, deprive ourselves of this diversion, for the very reason that it is agreeable; do a service to this disagreeable person, because he is disagreeable; take this bitter medicine, just because it is bitter. Self-love makes it appear to us that nothing is good in which we do not find our own satisfaction; but he that would wholly belong to God must do violence to himself whenever it is a question of anything pleasing to him and say always: "Let me lose everything, provided that I please God."

For the rest, no one is more contented in the world than he who despises all the goods of the world. Whoever strips himself the most of such goods becomes richest in divine graces. Thus does God know how to reward those who love Him faithfully.

But, O my Jesus, Thou knowest my weakness; Thou hast promised to help him who trusts in Thee. O Lord, I love Thee; in Thee I trust; give me strength, and make me entirely Thine own.

In Thee also I trust, O my sweet advocate, Mary.

Reflection 14

On the Necessity of
Mental Prayer

MENTAL prayer is necessary, in the first place, in order that we may have light on the journey we are making to eternity. The eternal truths are spiritual things, which are not seen with the eyes of the body, but only in the mind, by consideration. He that does not meditate, does not see them; therefore, he walks with difficulty on the way of salvation. And further, he who does not meditate, does not know his defects, and therefore, says St. Bernard, he does not detest them. So also, he does not see the dangers to salvation in which he is, and therefore does not think of avoiding them. But when anyone meditates, his defects and the dangers of losing his soul at once come before him; and seeing them, he will seek to remedy them. St. Bernard says that meditation regulates our affections, directs our actions and corrects our defects.

In the second place, without mental prayer we have not strength to resist temptations and practice virtues. St. Teresa used to say that when a man leaves off mental prayer, the devil has no need of carrying him to Hell, for he throws himself into it of his own accord. And the reason is that, without meditation, there is no prayer. God is most willing to give us His graces, but

St. Gregory says that, before giving them, He desires to be asked, and as it were, compelled to give them through our prayers. "God wants to be asked; He wants to be urged; He wants to be overcome by a certain importunity." But without prayer we shall not have strength to resist our enemies, and so we shall not obtain perseverance in virtue. Bishop Palafox, in his note upon the tenth letter of St. Teresa, writes thus: "How will God give us perseverance if we do not ask for it? And how shall we ask it without practicing mental prayer?" But he who practices meditation is "like a tree which is planted near the running waters, which shall bring forth its fruit in due season." (*Psalms* 1:3).

And further, meditation is the blessed furnace in which souls are inflamed with divine love: "In my meditation," says the Psalmist, "a fire shall flame out." (*Psalms* 38:4). St. Catherine of Bologna said: "Meditation is that bond which binds the soul to God." In the Sacred Canticles it is written: The King "brought me into the cellar of wine; he set in order charity in me." (*Canticle of Canticles* 2:4). This wine cellar is meditation, in which the soul becomes so inebriated with divine love that it loses, as it were, its feeling for the things of the world; it sees only that which pleases its Beloved; it speaks only of its Beloved; it would hear others speak only of its Beloved; every other discourse wearies and troubles it. In meditation, the soul retiring to converse alone with God is raised above itself. "He shall sit solitary and hold his peace," says the prophet. (*Lamentations* 3:28). When the soul sits solitary, that is, remains alone in meditation to consider how worthy God is of love and how great is the love He bears to it, it will there relish the sweetness of God and fill its mind with holy thoughts. There it will detach itself from earthly affections; there it will conceive great desires to become holy and finally resolve to give itself wholly to God.

And where have the Saints made those generous resolutions which have lifted them up to a sublime degree of perfection, if not in mental prayer?

Let us hear what St. John of the Cross said, speaking of mental prayer:

> He made me there upon His breast recline;
> There science sweet He did to me impart;
> There too I gave without reserve my heart,
> And pledged myself the spouse of Love Divine.

And St. Aloysius Gonzaga used to say that no one will ever attain a high degree of perfection who is not given to much mental prayer. Let us, then, attach ourselves to it and not leave it on account of any weariness that we may experience: this weariness which we endure for God will be abundantly recompensed by Him.

Pardon me, O my God, my slothfulness. What treasures of grace have I not lost by so often having given up mental prayer! For the future give me grace to be faithful in continuing to converse here on earth with Thee, with whom I hope to converse forever in Heaven. I do not ask Thee to favor me with Thy consolations in prayer; I do not deserve them; it is enough that Thou dost suffer me to remain at Thy feet to recommend to Thee my poor soul, which is poor indeed because it has wandered away from Thee. Here, O my crucified Jesus, the sole memory of Thy Passion shall keep me detached from earth and united with Thee.

O holy Virgin Mary, do thou assist me in prayer.

Reflection 15

The Ends of Mental Prayer

TO MAKE mental prayer well and derive from it great profit to the soul, we must determine the ends for which we intend to make it. First, we must meditate in order to unite ourselves more with God. It is not so much good thoughts in the mind as good acts of the will, or holy affections, which unite us with God; and such are the acts which we make in meditation—of humility, of confidence, of detachment, of resignation, and above all, of love and of repentance for our sins. The acts of love, says St. Teresa, are those which keep the heart inflamed with holy love.

Secondly, we must make mental prayer in order to obtain from God, by petitions, the graces which are necessary in order to enable us to advance in the way of salvation, and especially to obtain the divine light, in order to avoid sin and take the means which will lead us to perfection. The best fruit, therefore, of meditation is the exercise of the prayer of petition. Almighty God, ordinarily speaking, does not give graces to any but to those who pray. St. Gregory writes: "God desires to be entreated, He desires to be constrained, He desires to be conquered by a certain importunity." Observe His words, "to be conquered by importunity." At times, in order to obtain certain graces of special value, it will not suffice simply to pray, but it will be necessary to insist and, as it were, compel God by our prayers to give them to us. It is true that at all times He is ready to hear us, but at the time of meditation, when we are more recollected with God, He is more liberal in giving us His aid.

Above all, during meditation we must be careful to ask Him for perseverance and His holy love. Final perseverance is not one single grace, but a chain of graces, to which must correspond the chain of our prayers; if we cease to pray, God will cease to give us His help, and so we shall be lost. He who does not practice mental prayer will with difficulty persevere in God's grace till death. Bishop Palafox, in his note on St. Teresa's letters, writes thus: "How will the Lord give us perseverance if we do not ask Him for it? And how shall we ask for it without meditation? Without mental prayer, there is no communion with God."

Thus, likewise, must we be urgent with petitions to obtain from God His holy love. St. Francis de Sales used to say that with holy love all virtues come united. "All good things came to me together with her." (*Wisdom* 7:11). Let our prayer for perseverance and love, therefore, be continual; and in order to make it with greater confidence, let us ever bear in mind the promise made to us by Jesus Christ, that whatever we seek from God through the merits of His Son, He will give it to us. "Amen, amen, I say to you, if you ask the Father anything in My name, He will give it [to] you." (*John* 16:23). Let us then pray, and pray always, if we desire that God should make us abound in every blessing. Let us pray for ourselves; and if we have zeal for the glory of God, let us pray also for others. It is a thing most pleasing to God that we should pray to Him for unbelievers and heretics and all sinners. "Let people confess to Thee, O God; let all people give praise to Thee." (*Psalms* 66:4). Let us say: "O Lord, make them know

Thee, make them love Thee." We read in the lives of St. Teresa and St. Mary Magdalen de Pazzi how much God recommended these Saints to pray for sinners. And to our prayers for sinners, let us also add prayers for the Holy Souls in Purgatory.

Thirdly, we must go to meditation, not for the sake of spiritual consolations, but chiefly in order to learn in it what God requires of us. "Speak, Lord," let us say with Samuel, "for Thy servant heareth." (*1 Kings* 3:10). Lord, make me know what Thou wilt of me, and I will do it. Some persons continue meditation as long as consolations last, but when these cease, they leave off mental prayer. It is true that God is accustomed to console His beloved souls at the time of meditation and to give them some foretaste of the delights He prepares in Heaven for those who love Him. These are things which the lovers of the world do not comprehend; they who are accustomed to have no relish except for earthly delights despise those which are heavenly. Oh, if they had but experienced them, how surely would they leave all their pleasures to shut themselves in a cell to converse alone with God! Mental prayer is nothing else but a conversation between the soul and God: the soul pours forth to Him its affections, its desires, its fears, its petitions; and God speaks to the heart, causing it to know His goodness and the love which He bears it and what it has to do to please Him. "I . . . will lead her into the wilderness, and I will speak to her heart." (*Osee* 2:14).

But these delights are not always experienced; for the most part, holy souls suffer dryness in meditation. "By dryness and temptations," says St. Teresa, "the Lord makes trial of those who love Him." And she adds: "Even if this dryness lasts through life, let not the soul leave off mental prayer; the time will come when it will be very well paid for all." The time of dryness is the time of greatest pain. "Let us humble ourselves then and be resigned, seeing ourselves without fervor, without good desires, and as it were, unable to make a good act; let us humble ourselves, I say, and resign ourselves, for this very meditation will be more fruitful than others. It is enough then to say, if we can say nothing more, "O Lord, help me, have pity on me, abandon me not!" Let us also have recourse to our comfortress, the most holy Virgin Mary. Happy is he who does not leave off meditation when in desolation. God will make him abound in graces. Then let him say, "O my God, how can I expect to be consoled by Thee, I who at this hour should deserve to be in Hell, forever separated from Thee and deprived of all hope of being able to love Thee anymore!

I do not therefore complain, O my Lord, that Thou dost deprive me of Thy consolations; I do not deserve them, nor claim them. It is enough for me to know that Thou canst never reject a soul that loves Thee. Deprive me not of the power of loving Thee, and then treat me as Thou wilt. If it is Thy Will that I continue thus afflicted and desolate even till death, and through all eternity, I am content; it is enough if I can say with truth, "My God, I love Thee, I love Thee!"

Mary, Mother of God, have pity on me!

Reflection 16

On the Mercy of God

S O GREAT is the desire which God has to dispense to us His graces that, as St. Augustine says, He is more anxious to give them to us than we are desirous to receive them from Him. And the reason is that goodness, as philosophers say, is of its own nature diffusive; it is moved by its nature to diffuse itself in benefits to others. God, therefore, being infinite goodness, has an infinite desire to communicate Himself to us His creatures and make us share His goods.

Hence arises the great compassion which He has for our miseries. David says that the earth is full of the Divine Mercy. It is not full of the Divine Justice because God does not exercise His Justice in punishing evildoers, except when necessary and when He is, as it were, constrained to do so. On the contrary, He is bountiful and liberal in exercising His Mercy upon all, and at all times; whence St. James says: "Mercy exalteth itself above judgment." (*James* 2:13). Mercy frequently snatches from the Hand of Justice the scourges which are prepared for sinners and obtains their pardon. Therefore the prophet calls God by the very name of Mercy: "My God, my Mercy." (*Psalms* 58:18). And for the same reason he says, "For Thy name's sake, O Lord, Thou wilt pardon my sin." (*Psalms* 24:11). Lord, pardon me for Thy name's sake, for Thou art mercy itself.

Isaias said that chastisement is a work which is not according to the heart of God, but alien and foreign to it, as if he would say that it was far from His inclination. "The Lord . . . shall be angry . . . that He may do His work, His strange work; that He may perform His work, His work is strange to Him." (*Isaias* 28:21). In a word, His mercy it was that induced Him to send His own Son on earth to be made man and to die upon a cross to deliver us from eternal death. Therefore, Zachary exclaimed: "Through the bowels of the mercy of our God, in which the Orient from on high hath visited us." (*Luke* 1:78). The expression, "the bowels of the mercy of God," implies a mercy which proceeds from the depth of the heart of God, since He was content that His own Son-made-man should die, rather than that we should perish.

In order to see how great is the compassion of God for us and the desire He has to do us good, it is enough to read these few words which He says to us in the Gospel: "Ask, and it shall be given you." (*Luke* 11:9). What more could one friend say to another to show his affection? Ask me what you will, and I will give it to you. This is what God says to everyone of us. Seeing our misery, He invites us to come to Him and promises to relieve us: "Come to Me, all you that labor and are burdened, and I will refresh you." (*Matthew* 11:28). The Jews on one occasion complained of God and said they would no longer go to ask favors of Him; wherefore, He said to Jeremias: "Am I become a wilderness to Israel, or a lateward springing land? Why then have My people said: 'We are revolted; we will come to Thee no more?'" (*Jeremias* 2:31). At the same time, God was willing to prove the wrong which the Jews did to Him, since He always and immediately consoles everyone who has recourse to Him, as He said by Isaias: "As soon as He shall hear, He will answer Thee." (*Isaias* 30:19).

Art thou a sinner, and wilt thou have pardon? "Doubt not," says St. John Chrysostom, "for God has more desire to pardon thee than thou hast to be pardoned." If then God sees anyone obstinate in his sin, He waits in order to show him mercy, as Isaias says: "Therefore the Lord waiteth, that He may have mercy on you." (*Isaias* 30:18). And meantime He points out the chastisement that awaits him, in order that he may repent. "Thou hast given a warning to them that fear Thee, that they may flee from before the bow; that thy beloved may be delivered." (*Psalms* 59:6). At one time He stands and knocks at the door of our hearts, that we may open to Him: "Behold, I stand at the gate, and knock." (*Apocalypse* 3:20). At another, He entreats His people, saying, "Why will you die, O house of Israel?" (*Ezechiel* 18:31). As if He were saying, in compassion, "O my son, why wilt thou perish?" St. Dionysius the Areopagite writes, "God follows like a lover, even those who turn from Him, and entreats them not to perish." And this same thing was written before by the Apostle, when he implored sinners, on the part of Jesus Christ, to be reconciled with God, on which Chrysostom remarks: "Christ Himself is beseeching you, and what does He beseech you? That you would be reconciled to God."

If then some determine to continue obstinate, what more can God do? He makes all understand that whosoever comes to Him penitent, He will not drive him away: "Him that cometh to Me, I will not cast out." (*John* 6:37). He says that He is ready to embrace everyone who turns to Him: "Turn ye to Me . . . and I will turn to you." (*Zacharias* 1:3). He promises every wicked man that if he repents, He will pardon him and forget his sins. "If the wicked do penance, he shall live; I will not remember all his iniquities that he hath done." He even says: "Come, and accuse Me; . . . if your sins be as scarlet, they shall be made white as snow"

(*Isaias* 1:18)—as though He would say: "Come unto Me, repentant sinners, and if I embrace you not, reproach Me as one who had broken his word."

But no, the Lord knoweth not how to despise a contrite heart. "A contrite and humbled heart, O God, Thou wilt not despise." (*Psalms* 50:19). We read in St. Luke with what joy He embraced the lost sheep and with what love He welcomed the Prodigal Son when he returned to His feet. And Our Lord Himself adds: "I say to you that even so, there shall be joy in Heaven upon one sinner that doth penance, more than upon ninety-nine just who need not penance." (*Luke* 15:7). St. Gregory explains the reason for this by saying that, for the most part, penitent sinners are more fervent in loving God than those who, being innocent, have grown lukewarm in their security.

O my Jesus, since Thou hast had so great patience with me in waiting for me and so great love in pardoning me, as I trust, I resolve to love Thee very much; but it is Thou who must give me this love. Give it to me, O my Lord; little honor were it to Thee that I, a sinner so favored by Thee, should love Thee but little. O my Jesus, when shall I begin to be as grateful to Thee as Thou hast been gracious to me? In the past, instead of being grateful to Thee, I have offended and despised Thee. Shall I then hereafter always behave thus towards Thee, who hast spared nothing to gain my love? No, my Saviour, I will love Thee with all my heart, I resolve never to displease Thee. Thou dost command me to love Thee, and I desire nothing else but to love Thee. Thou dost seek me, and I seek nothing but Thee. Give me Thy help, without which I can do nothing.

O Mary, O Mother of mercy, draw me entirely to God.

Reflection 17

On Confidence in
Jesus Christ

WONDERFULLY great, as has been said, is the mercy of Jesus Christ to us; but for our greater good, He desires that we should hope in His mercy with a lively confidence, trusting in His merits and His promises. Therefore, St. Paul recommends to us this confidence, saying, "Do not therefore lose your confidence, which hath a great reward." (*Hebrews* 10:35). And therefore, when a fear of the Divine judgments seems to diminish this confidence in us, we ought to drive it away, and say to ourselves with the Psalmist: "Why art thou sad, O my soul, and why dost thou trouble me? Hope in God, for I will still give praise to Him, the salvation of my countenance and my God." (*Psalms* 41:6-7).

Our Lord revealed to St. Gertrude that our confidence offers such violence to Him that He cannot possibly refuse to hear us in everything we ask of Him. The same thing was said by St. John Climacus: "Prayer exercises a holy violence upon God." Every prayer offered with confidence, as it were, forces God, but this force is acceptable and pleasing to Him. Therefore, St. Bernard writes that the Divine Mercy is like an inexhaustible fountain, from which whosoever brings the larger vessel of confidence, carries away the greater abundance of graces. And this is according to what the Psalmist wrote: "Let Thy mercy, O Lord, be upon us, as we have hoped in Thee." (*Psalms* 32:22).

God has declared that He protects and saves all who trust in Him. Let all, then, rejoice, says David, who hope in Thee, my God; they shall be blessed forever, and Thou wilt ever dwell in them. (Cf. *Psalms* 5:12). The same prophet said: "Mercy shall encompass him that hopeth in the Lord." (*Psalms* 31:10). He that trusts in God shall be ever so encircled and guarded around that he will be safe from danger of perishing. Oh, what great promises the Holy Scriptures make to those who trust in God! Do we seem to be lost through the sins we have committed? Behold, the remedy at hand! "Let us go therefore with confidence," says the Apostle, "to the throne of grace, that we may obtain mercy and find grace in seasonable aid." (*Hebrews* 4:16). Let us not defer going to Jesus Christ until He is seated as Judge on His throne of Judgment; let us hasten at once, while He sits on His throne of grace. St. John Chrysostom says that our Saviour has a greater desire to pardon us than we have to be pardoned.

But, says some sinner, I do not deserve to be heard if I beg for pardon. I reply that though he has not deserved it, his confidence in the Divine Mercy will obtain grace for him, because this pardon is not dependent upon his merits, but upon the Divine promise to pardon those who repent; and this is what Jesus Christ says: "Everyone that asketh, receiveth." (*Matthew* 7:8). A learned author, commenting on the word "everyone," says that it means "everyone," whether just or sinner; it is sufficient that he pray with confidence. Let us, then, hear from the lips of Jesus Christ Himself what great things are done by confidence: "All things whatsoever you ask when you pray, believe that you shall receive, and they shall come unto you." (*Mark* 11:24).

Whosoever, then, fears that through weakness he will fall again into his old sins, let him trust in God, and he shall not fall, as the Psalmist assures us: "None of them that trust in Him shall offend." (*Psalms* 33:23). Isaias says that they who hope in the Lord renew their strength (*Isaias* 40:31); he means that they acquire a new strength. Let us, then, be firm in not wavering in our confidence, because God has promised, as St. Paul says, to protect all who hope in Him; and therefore, when anything seems especially difficult to overcome, let us say: "I can do all things in Him who strengtheneth me." (*Philippians* 4:13). And who that ever trusted in God was lost? "Know ye," says the Wise Man, "that no one hath hoped in the Lord, and hath been confounded." (*Ecclesiasticus* 2:11). Yet, let us not go about seeking always that sensible confidence we should wish to feel; it is enough if we have the will to trust. This is true confidence, the will to trust in God because He is good and desires to help us, and is powerful and can help us, and is faithful and has promised to help us. Above all, let us avail ourselves of the promise made by Jesus Christ: "Amen, amen, I say to you: if you ask the Father anything in My name, He will give it [to] you." (*John* 16:23). Thus, let us seek graces from God, through the merits of Jesus Christ, and we shall obtain whatever we will.

O Eternal God, I well know that I am poor in all things; I can do nothing, I have nothing, save what has come to me from Thy hands; therefore, all I say to Thee is, "Lord, have mercy upon me." The worst of it is that to my poverty I have added the sin of having abused Thy graces by the offenses I have committed against Thee. But notwithstanding all this, I will hope from Thy goodness this twofold mercy: first, that Thou wouldst give me holy perseverance, together with

Thy love and with the grace to pray to Thee always to help me, even till death. All this I ask of Thee, and I hope for it, through the merits of Thy Son Jesus and of the Blessed Virgin Mary.

O my Great Advocate, succor me with thy prayers.

Reflection 18

Salvation Alone Is Necessary

"ONE THING is necessary." It is not necessary that in this world we should be honored with dignities, that we should be provided with riches, with good health and with earthly pleasures; but it is necessary that we should be saved; for there is no middle course; if we are not saved, we must be damned. After this short life, we shall be either always happy in Heaven, or always miserable in Hell.

O my God, what will be my lot? Shall I be saved or lost? One lord or the other must necessarily be mine. I hope to be saved, but who assures me of it? I know that I have so many times deserved Hell. Jesus, my Saviour, Thy death is my hope.

How many persons are there in the world who were once upon a time loaded with riches and honors and lifted up to high positions, and even to thrones, and now find themselves in Hell, where all the fortune they enjoyed in this world serves only to increase their torments and despair! Behold the warning which Our Lord gives us: "Lay not up to yourselves treasures on earth . . . but lay up to yourselves treasures in Heaven, where neither the rust nor moth doth consume." (*Matthew* 6:19-20). Every gain of earthly goods is lost at death, but the gain of spiritual goods is an incomparable treasure and is eternal.

God has taught us that He "will have all men to be saved." (*1 Timothy* 2:4). And to all He gives the help needed for salvation. Miserable is he who is lost; it is entirely his own fault: "Destruction is thy own, O Israel; thy help is only in me." (*Osee* 13:9). And this will be the greatest torment of the poor reprobate, the thought that they are lost through their own fault. "The vengeance on the flesh of the ungodly," says the Scriptures, "is fire and worms." (*Ecclesiasticus* 7:19). Fire and worms, that is, the remorse of conscience, will be the torturers of the damned in punishment for their sins; but the worm will forever torment them, more terribly than the fire. How much regret we suffer in this world from the loss of any object of value—a diamond, a watch, a purse of money—when it happens through our own carelessness. We cannot eat or sleep for thinking of our loss, even though there is a hope of our repairing it in some other way. What then will be the torment of one who is lost, in thinking that, through his own fault he has lost God and Paradise, without a hope of ever being able to recover them!

"Therefore we have erred from the way of truth." (*Wisdom* 5:6). This will be the eternal lamentation of the miserable damned ones. "Therefore we have erred," losing our souls of our own accord, and there is no longer a remedy for our error! In all the misfortunes which occur to many in this life, a remedy is found in time either from a change of circumstances, or at least through a holy resignation to the will of God. But none of these remedies will be for us when we have reached eternity, if we have wandered from the way to Heaven.

Therefore, the Apostle St. Paul exhorts us to labor for eternal salvation with a continual fear of losing it: "With fear and trembling, work out your salvation." (*Philippians* 2:12). This fear will cause us always to walk with caution and fly from dangerous occasions;

it will make us continually recommend ourselves to God, and thus we shall be saved. Let us pray to Him, that he would make us fix firmly in our minds the thought that upon our last gasp of breath before death depends the question whether we shall be eternally happy or eternally miserable without hope of remedy.

My God, many times have I despised Thy grace; I should deserve no mercy; but Thy prophet tells me that "The Lord is good to . . . the soul that seeketh Him." (*Lamentations* 3:25). In the past I have fled from Thee; but now I seek nothing, I ask nothing, I love nothing but Thee. In pity, despise me not; remember the blood Thou hast shed for me.

This blood and thy intercession, O Mary, Mother of God, are all my hope.

Reflection 19

On Perfect Resignation to the Divine Will

"**M**Y MEAT is to do the will of Him that sent Me." (*John* 4:34). So said Jesus Christ, speaking of Himself. In this mortal life, meat is that which preserves our life, and therefore Our Lord said that it was His meat to do the will of the Father. This also ought to be the meat of our souls: "Life is in His good will." (*Psalms* 29:6). Our life consists in doing the Divine Will; he that does not fulfill it is dead.

The Wise Man says: "They that are faithful in love shall rest in Him," (*Wisdom* 3:9), that is to say, "shall acquiesce and submit to His will." They who are little faithful in loving God will desire that He should acquiesce with them, that He should conform Himself to their pleasure and do whatever they desire; but they who love God unite themselves with His Will and acquiesce in everything that God does with them and with all that concerns them. In every adversity which afflicts them, whether sickness, dishonor, annoyances, loss of property or of relations, they have ever on their lips and in their hearts: "Thy will be done," which is the usual aspiration of the Saints.

God desires only that which is best for us, namely, our sanctification. "This is the will of God," says the

Apostle, "your sanctification." (*1 Thessalonians* 4:3).
Let us take care, therefore, to subdue our own wills,
uniting them always to the will of God; and thus also
let us endeavor to control our minds, reflecting that
everything that God does is best for us. Whoever does
not act thus will never find true peace. All the perfection which can be attained in this world, which is
a place of purifications and consequently a place of
troubles and afflictions, consists in suffering patiently
those things which are opposed to our self-love; and
in order to suffer them with patience, there is no
means more efficacious than a willingness to suffer
them in order to do the will of God. "Submit thyself
then to Him, and be at peace." (*Job* 22:21). He that
acquiesces to the Divine Will in everything is always
at peace, and nothing of all that happens to him can
make him unhappy. "Whatsoever shall befall the just
man, it shall not make him sad." (*Proverbs* 12:21).
But why is the just man never miserable in any circumstances? Because he knows well that whatever
happens in the world happens through the will of
God.

The Divine Will (so to say) blunts the point of the
thorns and takes away the bitterness of the tribulations which come upon us in this world.

In the hymn on the Will of God, we say:

> Thou makest crosses soft and light,
> And death itself seem sweet and bright;
> No cross nor fear that soul dismays
> Whose will to Thee united stays.
>
> O Will of God! O Will Divine!
> All, all our love be ever Thine!

Behold the excellent counsel which St. Peter gives,
that we may find perfect peace in the midst of the

many trials of this present life: "Casting all your care upon Him, for He has care of you." (*1 Peter* 5:7). But if it is God who thus takes on Himself all thought for our welfare, why should we fret ourselves with so many anxieties, as if our welfare depended on our own efforts, and not rather abandon ourselves into the hands of God, upon whom all depends? "Cast thy care upon the Lord," says David, "and He shall sustain thee." (*Psalms* 54:23). Let us be attentive to obey God in everything He commands and counsels us, and then let us leave to Him the care of our salvation, and He will remember to give us all the means which are necessary, in order that we may be saved. Whosoever places his whole confidence in God is sure of eternal salvation.

In a word, whoever does the Will of God enters into Paradise; and he that does it not, enters not. Some people trust their eternal salvation to certain devotions, or to certain outward works of piety, and yet will not do the Will of God. But Jesus Christ says: "Not everyone that saith to Me, 'Lord, Lord,' shall enter into the kingdom of heaven; but he that doth the will of My father who is in heaven, he shall enter into the kingdom of heaven." (*Matthew* 7:21).

Thus, if we desire to be saved and to acquire a perfect union with God, we should endeavor always to address to Him the prayer of David: "Teach me to do Thy will, for Thou art my God." (*Psalms* 142:10). And meanwhile, let us strip ourselves of our own will and give it wholly to God without reserve. When we give to God our goods by alms, our food by fasting, our blood by scourging, we give Him what we possess; but when we give Him our will, we give Him ourselves altogether. Wherefore he that gives to God his entire will is able to say: "Lord, having given Thee all my will, I have nothing more to give Thee." The sacrifice of our own will is the most acceptable sacrifice we can make to God; and God pours His graces abundantly upon him who makes it.

This sacrifice, however, in order to be perfect, must have two conditions: it must be without reserve, and it must be constant. Some persons give to God their will, but with a certain reserve; and this gift pleases God but little. Others give Him their will, but they afterwards take it back again; and such persons place themselves in great peril of being abandoned by God. Therefore, it is necessary that all our efforts and desires and prayers should be directed to obtain from God perseverance in not willing anything but what He wills. Let us then, day by day, renew the total renunciation of our own will to God and constantly take care to seek and wish for nothing which is not according to the Will of God. And thus will cease within us our passions, desires and fears, and all our disordered affections. Sister Margaret of the Cross, a daughter of the Emperor Maximilian and a barefooted Poor Clare, when she became quite blind, was accustomed to say: "How can I desire to see, when God wills it not?"

Receive, O God of my soul, receive the sacrifice of my entire will and of all my liberty. I see that I deserve that Thou shouldst turn Thy back upon me and refuse this gift of mine, so often have I been unfaithful to Thee; but I hear Thee once more command me to love Thee with all my heart, and therefore I am sure that Thou dost accept it. I resign myself, then, wholly to Thy will; make me know what Thou dost will of me, for I resolve to accomplish it all. Make me love Thee, and then dispose of me and all that is mine as it pleases Thee. I am in Thy hands; do what Thou knowest to be most expedient for my eternal salvation; meanwhile, I declare that I desire Thee alone and nothing more.

O Mother of God, do thou obtain for me holy perseverance.

> O Jesus, my beloved Lord,
> I seek for nought but Thee!
> My God, to Thee I give myself,
> Do what Thou wilt with me.

Reflection 20

Blessed Is He who Is
Faithful to God in Adversity

THE fidelity of soldiers is proved, not indeed in repose, but in action. This earth is for us a battlefield where everyone has to fight and conquer in order to be saved; if he does not conquer, he is lost forever. Therefore said holy Job: "All the days in which I am now in warfare, I expect until my change come." (*Job* 14:14). Job suffered in struggling with ever so many enemies, but he comforted himself with the hope that, conquering and rising again after death, he would change his state. Of this change St. Paul spoke and rejoiced, saying: "The dead shall rise again incorruptible, and we shall be changed." (*1 Corinthians* 15:52). Our state is changed in Heaven, which is a place of no more toil, but of rest; not of fear, but of security; not of sadness or weariness, but of gladness and joy eternal. With the hope then of such great joy, let us animate ourselves to fight until death and never give ourselves up conquered to our enemies, "until our change come," until our struggle is ended and we possess a blessed eternity.

"The patient man shall bear for a time, and afterwards joy shall be restored to him." (*Ecclesiasticus* 1:29). Blessed is he who suffers for God in this life; he suffers "for a time," but his joy will be eternal in the country of the Blessed. Thus will end the persecutions; the temptations will end; the infirmities, the annoyances and all the miseries of this life will end; and God will give us a life of complete happiness, which shall never end. Now is the time for pruning the vine and for cutting off everything which hinders us on our way towards the promised land of Heaven. "The time of pruning is come." (*Canticle of Canticles* 2:12). But cutting off causes pain, so that we have need of patience; and then "afterwards joy shall be restored," when the more we have suffered, the more shall we be filled with consolations. God is faithful! And to him who suffers with resignation on earth for His love's sake, He promises that He Himself will be his reward, a reward infinitely greater than all our suffering: "I am thy protector and thy reward exceeding great." (*Genesis* 15:1)

Meanwhile, before we receive the crown of eternal life, the Lord wills that we should be tried by temptations. "Blessed is the man that endureth temptation; for when he hath been proved, he shall receive the crown of life, which God hath promised to them that love Him." (*James* 1:12). Blessed then is he who is faithful to God when suffering adversity. Some people think they are beloved of God when all their temporal affairs go prosperously and they have no troubles; but they are mistaken, because God does not try the patience and faithfulness of His servants by prosperity, but by adversity, in order to give them that crown which fades not away, as all the crowns of this earth do fade away. This shall be a crown of eternal glory, as St. Peter writes: "You shall receive a never-fading crown of glory." (*1 Peter* 5:4). To whom, then, is this crown promised? St. James says: "God has promised it to them that love Him." (*James* 1:12). God has promised it again and again to those who love Him, because divine love will make us fight with courage and win the victory.

To love of God we must also join humility. The Word of God says, "Gold and silver are tried in the fire, but acceptable men in the furnace of humiliation. (*Ecclesiasticus* 2:5). It is in humiliations that Saints are discovered, for *there* is made known whether they are gold or lead. Such a one is considered a saint; but when he receives an injury from another, he is entirely disturbed; he complains of it to everyone; he says he will make him repent of it. What does this show? It is a sign that he is not gold, but lead. The Lord says, "In thy humiliation keep patience." (*Ecclesiasticus* 2:4). The proud man, whatever humiliation he receives, considers it a great injustice, and therefore cannot endure it; the humble man, on the contrary, accounting himself deserving of every evil treatment, suffers all with patience. Let him who has committed one mortal sin cast a glance upon the Hell which he has deserved, and thus will he suffer with patience every contempt and every pain.

Let us then love God; let us be humble; and whatever we do, let us do it, not to please ourselves, but only to please God. O accursed self-love, which intrudes itself into all our works! Even in our spiritual exercises, in meditation, in works of penance, and in all our pious works, it goes seeking its own interests. Few are the devout souls who do not fall into this defect: "Who shall find a valiant woman? Far and from the uttermost coasts is the price of her." (*Proverbs* 31:10). Where shall we find a soul so valiant that, despoiled of every passion and of all self-interest, it continues to love Jesus Christ in the midst of slights, pains, desolations of spirit and the annoyances of life? Solomon says that such souls are gems of great price; they come from the farthest ends of the world and therefore are most rare. (*Proverbs* 31:10 ff.).

O my crucified Jesus, I am one of those who, even in my devotions, have been seeking my own pleasure and my own satisfaction; entirely unlike to Thee, who through love of me, hast led a life of tribulations, deprived of every alleviation. Give me Thy help, since from this day forward I will seek only Thy pleasure and Thy glory. I wish to love Thee without any interested motive; but I am weak, Thou must give me the strength to accomplish it. Behold me, I am Thine; dispose of me as it pleases Thee; make me love Thee, and I ask for nothing more.

O Mary, my Mother, obtain for me faithfulness to God through thy intercession.

Reflection 21

He that Loves Jesus Christ Ought to Hate the World

WHOSOEVER loves Jesus with a true love rejoices sincerely when he sees himself treated by the world as Jesus Christ was treated, who was hated, reviled and persecuted by the world, even to make Him die of anguish upon a gibbet of infamy.

The world is completely against Jesus Christ, and therefore, hating Jesus Christ, it hates all His servants. Therefore, Our Lord encouraged His disciples to suffer in peace the persecutions of the world, saying to them that, having given up the world, they could not but be hated by the world. "You are not of the world . . . therefore the world hateth you." (*John* 15:19).

Now, as the lovers of God are hateful to the world, so the world ought to be hateful to him who loves God. St. Paul says, "God forbid that I should glory, save in the cross of our Lord Jesus Christ, by whom the world is crucified to me." (*Galatians* 6:14). The Apostle was an object of horror to the world, as is a man condemned and dead upon a cross; and thus in return, the world was an object of horror to St. Paul: "the world is crucified to me." (*Galatians* 6:14).

Jesus Christ chose to die crucified for our sins for this end, that He might deliver us from the love of

77

this wicked world. Our Saviour, having called us to His love, desires that we should become superior to all the promises and threats of the world. He desires that we should no longer take account of its censures or of its praises. We must beg of God to make us utterly forget the world and to make us rejoice when we see the world reject us.

However, it is not enough, in order to belong wholly to God, that we should abandon the world; we must desire that the world should abandon us and utterly forget us. Some people leave the world, but they do not cease to wish to be praised by it, at least for having abandoned it; in such persons the desire of the esteem of the world is yet living and causes the world still to live in them.

So then, as the world hates the servants of God and therefore hates their good example and holy maxim, so also it is necessary that we should hate all the maxims of the world. "The wisdom of the flesh is an enemy to God, for it is not subject to the law of God, neither can it be." (*Romans* 8:7). The Apostle says, "Neither can it be." Yes, because the world has no other object but its own interest or pleasure, and thus it cannot agree with those who seek only to please God.

Yes, my Jesus, crucified and dead for me! Thee alone I desire to please. What is the world to me? What are riches, what are honors? Thou, my Redeemer, Thou shalt be all my treasure; to love Thee is my riches. If Thou wilt have me poor, I desire to be poor; if Thou wilt have me humbled and despised by all, I embrace everything and receive it from Thy hands; Thy will shall ever be my consolation. This is the grace that I seek of Thee, that in every event I may not depart in the least thing from Thy holy Will.

Reflection 22

The Words of a Dying Man to Jesus Crucified

O JESUS, my Redeemer, who in a few moments wilt be my Judge, have mercy upon me before the moment comes when Thou wilt judge me. No, my sins do not terrify me, nor the rigors of Thy judgment, while I see Thee dead upon this cross to save me.

Yet, cease not to comfort me in the agony to which I am come: my enemies would terrify me by saying that there is no salvation for me; "Many say to my soul, there is no salvation for him in his God." (*Psalms* 3:3). But I will never cease to trust in Thy goodness and say, "Thou, O Lord, art . . . the lifter up of my head." (*Psalms* 3:3). Do Thou comfort me; do Thou make me feel that Thou art my salvation; "Say to my soul, I am thy salvation." (*Psalms* 34:3). Oh, let not so many pains, so many insults endured, so much blood shed by Thee, be lost to me; "Thou hast redeemed me, dying upon the cross; let not so great labor be in vain." Especially, I pray Thee—through that bitterness Thou didst feel when Thy blessed soul was separated from Thy most holy body—to have mercy upon my soul when it shall depart from my body.

It is true that by my sins I have so often despised Thee, but now I love Thee above everything; I love Thee more than myself, and I grieve with all my heart

for all the outrages I have offered Thee; I detest them,
I hate them above all evil. I see that by the offenses
I have committed, I have deserved a thousand Hells;
but the bitter death which Thou hast been willing to
endure for me and the great mercies Thou hast already
shown me make me confidently hope that, when I
appear before Thee, Thou wilt give me the holy kiss
of peace.

Trusting entirely in Thy goodness, O my God, I abandon myself into Thy loving arms. "In Thee, O Lord, I
have hoped: I shall not be confounded forever." (*Psalms*
30:1). By the sins I have committed I have again and
again deserved Hell but I hope in Thy blood that Thou
hast already pardoned me; and I hope that I shall come
to Heaven to praise Thy mercies forever; "The mercies
of the Lord I will sing forever."

I willingly accept all the pains Thou dost destine for
me in Purgatory; it is just that the fire should punish
in me all the injuries I have done to Thee. O holy
prison, when shall I find myself shut up in thee, secure
from being able ever to lose my God! O holy fire, when
wilt thou purge away my many filthy stains and make
me worthy to enter the country of the blessed!

O Eternal Father, through the merits of the death
of Thy Son, Jesus Christ, make me die in Thy grace
and in Thy love, that I may come to love Thee eternally. I thank Thee for all the graces Thou hast given
me throughout my life and especially for the great
favor of having bestowed on me the Holy Faith and
for having caused me to receive, in these my last days,
all the holy Sacraments. Thou willest that I should
die, and I desire to die to please Thee. It is little, O
Jesus, my Saviour, that I should die for Thee, who hast
died for me. Joyfully I say to Thee with St. Francis:
"May I die for love of Thy love, who hast vouchsafed
to die for love of my love."

I receive death with peace, as also the pains which I shall have to endure as long as I breathe; give me strength to suffer with a perfect uniformity to Thy Will. I offer them all for Thy glory, uniting them to the pains which Thou didst suffer in Thy Passion. O Eternal Father, I sacrifice to Thee my life and my entire being; and I pray Thee to accept this my sacrifice, through the merits of that great sacrifice which Jesus, Thy Son, offered of Himself to Thee upon the Cross.

O Mother of God and my mother, Mary, thou hast obtained so many graces from God for me during my life; I thank thee for them with all my heart. Oh, abandon me not in this hour of my death, in which I have yet greater need of thy prayers! Pray to Jesus for me; increase thy prayers and obtain for me more sorrow for my sins and more love for God, that I may come to love Him forever in thy company and with all my powers in Heaven.

"In thee, O Lady, I have hoped; I shall not be confounded forever." Mary, my hope, I trust in thee.

Reflection 23

Acts to Be Made at Death

I T WAS revealed to St. Lydwina [of Schiedam, 1380-1433] by an angel that the crown of merits and glory which awaited her in Heaven would not be completed without the sufferings which she was to endure in the days immediately preceding her death. The same thing happens to all devout souls when they depart from this world. It is certain that all good acts, and especially those of resignation in accepting death, performed with the view of pleasing God, are of great merit to everyone who dies in the grace of God. Here are the acts of devotion which may be very acceptable to Almighty God at the time of death.

O my God, I offer Thee my life, and I am prepared to die at any hour which may be pleasing to Thy holy will. "Thy will be done." Always, always, "Thy will be done!"

O Lord, if Thou willest to leave me in life for some time longer, be Thou blessed; but I desire not life, unless I have to spend it all in loving Thee and in giving Thee pleasure. If Thou willest that I should die of this sickness, mayest Thou still be blessed. I embrace death that I may do Thy will, and I repeat: "Thy will be done, Thy will be done." I only beg of Thee to help me all through this time. "Have mercy on me, O God, according to Thy great mercy." If, then, Thou willest that I should leave this earth, I protest that I desire to die, because such is Thy will.

And I desire to die, in order that, by the anguish and bitterness of my death, I may satisfy Thy Divine Justice for so many sins by which I have offended Thee and deserved Hell.

I also desire to die that I may never more offend Thee, or cause Thee displeasure in this life.

Moreover, I desire to die in acknowledgment of the gratitude which I owe Thee for so many benefits and kindnesses that Thou hast bestowed on me, contrary to my deserts.

I desire to die that I may prove that I love Thy will more than my life.

I desire, if it pleases Thee, to die now, when I trust I am in Thy grace, in order to be assured that I shall praise and bless Thee forever.

I desire above all to die in order that I may come to love Thee eternally and with all my powers in Heaven, where through Thy blood, O my Redeemer, I hope to come and to be safe from ever ceasing to love Thee through all eternity. O my Jesus, Thou didst accept the death of the cross through love of me; I accept death and all the pains which await me through love of Thee. Meanwhile, I say with St. Francis: "May I die, O Lord, for the love of Thy love, who didst deign to die for the love of my love."

I pray Thee, O my Saviour, my Love, and my only Good, by Thy holy wounds and Thy bitter death, make me die in Thy grace and in Thy love. Thou hast purchased me with Thy blood; suffer me not to perish. O sweetest Jesus, suffer me not to be separated from Thee; suffer me not to be separated from Thee!

O Lord, cast me not away from Thy face. I confess that by my sins I have deserved Hell, but I grieve for them more than for any other evil; and I hope to come to Heaven to praise forever these great mercies Thou hast shown me. "The mercies of the Lord I will sing forever."

I adore Thee, O my God, who hast created me. I believe in Thee, O Eternal Truth. I hope in Thee, O Infinite Mercy. I love Thee, O Supreme Goodness; I love Thee above everything; I love Thee more than myself, for Thou art worthy of being loved. And because I love Thee, I repent with all my heart for having despised Thy grace. I promise Thee to suffer every kind of death, and a thousand deaths, rather than displease Thee again.

O Jesus, Son of God, who didst die for me, have pity upon me! My Saviour, save me; and let it be my salvation to love Thee eternally.

O Mary, Mother of God, pray to Jesus for me; now is the time in which thou hast most to help me. Mary, Mother of grace, Mother of mercy, defend us from the enemy and receive us in the hour of death. "We fly to thy patronage, O holy Mother of God! Holy Mary, Mother of God, pray for us sinners!"

St. Joseph, my patron and my father, help me at this time. St. Michael the Archangel, deliver me from the devils who lie in wait for my soul. O my holy advocates, and all ye Saints of Paradise, pray to God for me.

And Thou, my Crucified Jesus, at the moment when I must breathe my last, receive my soul into Thy arms; to Thee I recommend it; remember that Thou hast redeemed me with Thy blood. "We therefore pray Thee, help Thy servants whom Thou hast redeemed with Thy precious blood." O my Crucified Jesus, my love, and my hope, whether I live or die, I protest that I desire Thee alone and nothing more. Thou art my God and my all, and what else can I desire but Thee! "What have I in Heaven? And besides Thee, what do I desire upon earth? . . . Thou art the God of my heart and the God that is my portion forever!" (*Psalms* 72:25-26). Thou art the Love of my heart; Thou art all my riches!

To Thee, then, I recommend my soul—to Thee, who hast redeemed it by Thy death. "Into Thy hands, O Lord, I commend my spirit: Thou hast redeemed me, O Lord, the God of truth." (*Psalms* 30:6). Trusting in Thy mercy, I therefore say, "In Thee, O Lord, have I hoped; I shall not be confounded forever." (*Psalms* 30:1). O Mary, thou art my hope; "Hail, our hope!" To thee, therefore, I say again, "In thee, O Lady, have I hoped; I shall not be confounded forever."

Reflection 24

On the House of Eternity

"**M**AN SHALL go into the house of his eternity." (*Ecclesiastes* 12:5). We err in calling this habitation in which we now dwell our home. The home of our body in a little while will be a grave, in which it must rest until the Day of Judgment; and the home of the soul will be either Paradise or Hell, according as it has deserved, and there will it remain through all eternity.

At our burial, our corpses will not go to the grave of themselves; they will be carried there by others; but the soul will go of itself to the place which awaits it, either of eternal joy or eternal woe. "Man shall go into the house of his eternity." According as a man lives well or ill, so he goes of himself to his home in Paradise or in Hell, which habitation he shall never change.

Those who live on this earth often change their dwelling, either to please themselves or because they are compelled. In eternity the dwelling is never changed; where we enter at first, there we abide forever. "If the tree fall to the south or to the north, in what place soever it shall fall, there shall it be." (*Ecclesiastes* 11:3). He that enters in the south, which is Heaven, will be ever happy; he that enters in the north, which is Hell, will be ever miserable.

He, then, who enters Heaven will be always united

with God, always in company with the Saints, always in perfect peace, always fully satisfied, because every blessed soul is filled and satiated with joy, nor will he ever know the fear of losing it. If fear of losing the happiness they enjoy could enter among the Blessed, they would be no longer Blessed, for the mere thought of losing the joy they possess would disturb the peace they enjoy.

On the contrary, whoever enters into Hell will be forever far from God; he will be ever suffering in the fire among the damned. Let us not think that the pains of Hell will be like those of earth, where, by the effect of habit, a pain grows less; for, as in Paradise the delights will never cause weariness, but seem ever new as though they were for the first time enjoyed (which is implied by the expression of "the new canticle," which the blessed are ever singing); so on the contrary, in Hell, the pains never diminish their torment. The miserable beings who are damned will feel the same agony through all eternity which they felt in the first moment they experienced the pains of Hell.

St. Augustine used to say that he who believes in eternity and is not converted to God has either lost his reason or his faith. "Woe," cries St. Cæsarius, "woe to sinners who enter eternity without knowing what it is through having neglected to think upon it." And then he adds, "But, O double woe! They enter it, and they never come forth." It is a double woe, the first of which will be to fall into that abyss of fire; the second, that he who falls into it will never come out: the gate of Hell opens only to those who enter, not to those who would go out.

No, the Saints did not do too much when they went to hide themselves in caves and deserts, to live upon herbs and sleep on the ground in order to save their souls. No, "They did not do too much," says St. Bernard, "because, where eternity is in question, no security can be too great." When therefore God visits us with any cross of sickness, poverty or other trial, let us think of the Hell we have deserved, and thus every affliction will appear light. Let us say, with Job: "I have sinned, and indeed I have offended, and I have not received what I deserved." (*Job* 33:27). O Lord, I have offended Thee and so many times betrayed Thee, and I have not been punished as I deserved; how, then, can I complain if Thou sendest me some affliction—I, who have deserved Hell?

O my Jesus, send me not to Hell, for in Hell I could no longer love Thee, but would have to hate Thee forever. Deprive me of everything—of goods, of health, of life—but deprive me not of Thyself. Grant that I may love Thee and praise Thee forever, and then chastise me and do with me what Thou wilt.

O Mother of God, pray to Jesus for me.

Reflection 25

Souls that Greatly Love God Long to Go and Behold Him in Heaven

"WHILE we are in the body, we are absent from the Lord," says the Apostle. (*2 Corinthians* 5:6). Souls who in this life love nothing but God are like noble pilgrims, destined, according to their present state, to be the eternal spouse of the King of Heaven, but who now live at a distance without seeing Him. Wherefore, they do nothing but sigh for their departure to the country of the Blessed, where they know that their Spouse awaits them.

They know indeed that their Beloved is ever present with them, but He is as it were hidden behind a curtain and does not show Himself. Or rather, He is as the sun is frequently, behind clouds, through which, from time to time, it sends forth some ray of its splendor, but does not display itself openly. Moreover, these beloved spouses have a bandage over their eyes, which prevents them from seeing the object of their love. They live, nevertheless, contented, uniting themselves to the will of their Lord, who chooses to keep them in exile and far away from Himself; but with all this, they cannot but continually sigh to behold Him face to face, in order to become more charmed and more inflamed with love for Him.

Therefore, each one of them often sweetly complains to its beloved Spouse because He does not show Himself and says: "O Thou only Love of my heart, since Thou dost love me so much and hast wounded me with Thy holy love, why dost Thou hide Thyself and dost not let me see Thee? I know that Thou art an Infinite Beauty; I love Thee more than myself, though I have never yet beheld Thee. Show me Thy beautiful countenance; I long to see Thee unveiled, so that I may no longer behold myself nor any creature and may think only of loving Thee, my Sovereign Good."

When to these souls thus enamored of God there shines forth any ray of the Divine Goodness and of the love which God bears them, they would wish to be dissolved and melt away for desire of Him; and yet for them the sun is still behind the clouds, and His fair face is concealed behind a veil, and there is still the bandage over their eyes, so that they cannot gaze on Him face to face. But what will be their joy when the clouds shall disperse, when the veil shall be withdrawn, and the bandage shall be taken from their eyes, and the fair countenance of their Spouse shall appear unveiled, so that in the clear light they shall see His beauty, His goodness, His greatness and the love which He bears to them!

O death, why dost thou so long delay to come? If thou comest not, I cannot depart to behold my God. It is thou who must open to me the gate, that I may enter into the palace of my Lord. O blessed country, when will the day come in which I shall find myself within thine eternal tabernacles?

O Beloved of my soul, my Jesus, my Treasure, my Love, my All, when shall come that happy moment when, leaving this earth, I shall see myself entirely united to

Thee? I deserve not this happiness; but the love which Thou hast shown me, and still more Thine Infinite Goodness, make me hope that I shall be one day joined to those happy souls who, being wholly united to Thee, love Thee, and will love Thee with a perfect love through all eternity. O my Jesus, Thou seest the alternative in which I am placed, of being either forever united to Thee, or forever banished far from Thee. Have pity upon me; Thy blood is my hope!

And thy intercession, O my mother Mary, is my comfort and my joy!

Reflection 26

Jesus Is the Good Shepherd

THUS He Himself spoke: "I am the good Shepherd." (*John* 10:11). The office of a good shepherd is none other than to guide his flock to good pastures and to guard them from wolves; but what shepherd, O my sweet Redeemer, ever had goodness like to Thine, who didst give Thy life to save Thy sheep, which we are, and to deliver us from the punishment we had deserved?

St. Peter says of Jesus: "Who his own self bore our sins in His body upon the tree, that we, being dead to sins, should live to justice, by whose stripes we were healed." (*1 Peter* 2:24). To heal us of our ills, this good Shepherd took upon Himself all our debts and paid them in His own body, dying with agony upon a cross. It was this excess of love toward us His sheep which made St. Ignatius the martyr burn with desire to give his life for Jesus Christ, saying: "My Love is crucified," as he wrote in his epistle, as though he would say, "What! Has my God been willing to die on a cross for me, and can I live and not desire to die for Him?" And in truth, what great thing did the martyrs do in giving their lives for Jesus Christ, who died for love of them? Oh how the death endured for them by Jesus Christ made sweet to them all their torments—the scourges, the racks, the hooks, the red-hot plates of iron and the most painful deaths!

But the love of this Good Shepherd was not satisfied with giving His life for His sheep; He desired also, after His death, to leave them His very body itself, already first sacrificed on the Cross, that it might be the food and pasture of their souls. "The burning love which He bore to us," says St. John Chrysostom, "induced Him to unite Himself to us, in order to make Himself one thing with us, for such is the instinctive desire of ardent lovers."

And then, when this Good Shepherd sees one of His sheep lost, what does He not do, what means does He not take, to recover it? And He does not cease to seek it till He finds it. "If He shall lose one of them," says Our Lord in the Gospel, "He goes after that which was lost until He finds it." And when He has found it, rejoicing, He places it upon His shoulders, that He may not lose it again; and calling to Him His friends and neighbors, that is, the Angels and Saints, He invites them to rejoice with Him for having recovered the sheep that was lost. Who then will not love with all his affections this good Lord, who shows Himself thus loving to sinners who have turned their backs upon Him and lost themselves of their own accord!

O my amiable Saviour, behold at Thy feet a lost sheep! I have left Thee, but Thou has not abandoned me. Thou hast left no means untried to recover me. What would have become of me if Thou hadst not thought of seeking me? Unhappy me! How long have I not lived far from Thee! Now, through Thy mercy, I trust that I am in Thy grace; and though formerly I fled from Thee, now I desire nothing but to love Thee and to live and die embracing Thy feet. But as long as I live, I am in danger of leaving Thee. Oh bind me, bind me fast with the chains of Thy holy love, and cease not to seek me for so long as I live on this earth.

"I have gone astray like a sheep that is lost; seek Thy servant." (*Psalms* 118:176).

O Advocate of Sinners, obtain for me holy perseverance.

On the Business of Eternal Salvation

THE business of our eternal salvation is for us that affair which is not only the most important, but the only one which ought to trouble us, because if this goes wrong, all is lost. One thought upon eternity, well weighed, is enough to make a saint. The great servant of God, Fr. Vincent Carafa, was accustomed to say that, if all men thought with a lively faith upon the eternity of the next life, the world would become a desert, for no one would attend any more to the affairs of this life.

Oh, that all had ever before their eyes the great maxim taught us by Jesus Christ: "What doth it profit a man, if he gain the whole world, and suffer the loss of his own soul?" (*Matthew* 16:26). This maxim has induced so many men to leave the world, so many noble virgins, even of royal blood, to shut themselves up in a cloister, so many anchorites [hermits] to live in deserts, and so many martyrs to give their lives for the Faith, because they considered that, if they lost their souls, all the goods of the world would profit them nothing in eternity.

Therefore the Apostle wrote to his disciples: "We entreat you, brethren, . . . that you do your own business." (*1 Thessalonians* 4:11). And of what business did

St. Paul speak? He spoke of that business which, if it fail, implies that we lose the eternal kingdom of Paradise and are cast into an abyss of torments which never end. "It is an affair of eternal punishments and of the loss of the heavenly kingdom," says St. John Chrysostom.

St. Philip Neri, therefore, had good reason for calling all those persons mad who in this life take pains to gain riches and honors and give little heed to the salvation of their souls. "All such," the venerable John Avila used to say, "deserve to be shut up in an asylum for lunatics." How so? This great servant of God meant to say: "You believe that there is an eternity of joys for those who love God and an eternity of pain for those who offend Him, and do you offend Him?"

Every loss of goods, of reputation, of relations, of health in this life can be repaired, at least by a good death and by the acquisition of eternal life, as it happened to the holy martyrs; but for what goods of the world, for what fortune, even the greatest, can be given in exchange the loss of the soul? "What exchange shall a man give for his soul?" (*Matthew* 16:26).

He who dies in the enmity of God and loses his soul, loses with it forever all hope of repairing his ruin. "When the wicked man is dead, there shall be no hope any more." (*Proverbs* 11:7). O God, if the doctrine of eternal life were but simply a doubtful opinion of divines, we ought surely to give all our care to gain a happy eternity and avoid a miserable one. But no, it is not a doubtful thing; it is certain, it is of faith that one or the other must be our lot!

But what do we see? Everyone who has faith, and thinks upon this truth says: "So it is: we must attend to the salvation of our soul," but few are they who do attend to it in earnest. All are intent on gaining some lawsuit or obtaining some situation, but lay aside the care of their eternal salvation. "Truly, it is the greatest of errors to neglect the business of eternal salvation," said St. Eucherius. It is an error which exceeds all others, for to lose the soul is an error without remedy. "Oh, that they would be wise and would understand and would provide for their last end!" Miserable are those learned men who know many things and know not how to have any forethought for their souls, that they may obtain a favorable sentence in the Day of Judgment!

O my Redeemer, Thou hast shed Thy blood to purchase my soul, and I have so often lost it, and lost it again! I give Thee thanks that Thou hast given me time to recover it by recovering Thy grace. O my God, would that I had died before I had ever offended Thee! It comforts me to know that Thou knowest not how to despise a heart which humbles itself, and repents of its sins.

O Mary, Refuge of Sinners, succor a sinner who recommends himself to thee and trusts in thee.

Reflection 28

What Will Be the Happiness of the Blessed

"ENTER thou into the joy of thy Lord." (*Matthew* 25:23). When the soul enters the Country of the Blessed and the curtain which hinders its sight is taken away, it will see openly and without a veil the infinite beauty of its God, and this will be the joy of the Blessed.

Every object which then it will see in God Himself will overwhelm it with delight: it will see the righteousness of His judgments, the harmony of His decrees regarding every soul, all directed to His own divine glory and the good of each soul.

It will especially perceive, in respect to itself, the boundless love which God has entertained toward it in becoming man and sacrificing His life upon the Cross through love of it. Then will it know what an excess of goodness is contained in the mystery of the Cross, in the sight of God-become-a-servant and dying crucified upon an infamous gibbet, and in the mystery of the Eucharist, in the sight of God concealed beneath the species of bread and become the food of His creatures.

The soul will perceive in particular all the graces and favors bestowed on it, which until then had been hidden. It will see all the mercies He has shown it in waiting for it and pardoning its ingratitude. It will see the many calls and lights and aids which have been granted to it in abundance. It will see that those tribulations, those infirmities, those losses of property or of kindred, which it regarded as punishments, were not really punishments, but loving dispensations on the part of God to draw it to a perfect love for Him.

In a word, all these things will make known to it the infinite goodness of its God and the boundless love which He deserves. Hence, no sooner will it have reached Heaven than its sole desire will be to see Him blessed and happy; and at the same time, comprehending that the happiness of God is supreme, infinite and eternal, it will experience only a joy which is not infinite, because a creature is not capable of anything infinite. It will enjoy, nevertheless, a delight which is immense and complete, and will fill it with joy, and with that same joy which belongs to God Himself; and thus will be fulfilled in it the words: "Enter thou into the joy of thy Lord." (*Matthew* 25:23).

The Blessed are happy, not so much through the delight which they experience in themselves, as through the happiness which God enjoys. For as the Blessed love God immensely more than themselves, so the well-being of God delights them immensely more than their own on account of the love which they bear to Him. And this love for God will make them forget themselves, and all their delight will be to please their Beloved.

And this is that holy and loving inebriation which causes the Blessed to lose all thought of themselves, to occupy themselves solely in praising and loving the Dear Object of all their love, which is God. "They shall be inebriated with the plenty of Thy house." (*Psalms* 35:9). Happy from their first entrance into Heaven, they continue, as it were, "lost," and so to say, "drowned" in love, in that boundless ocean of the goodness of God.

Wherefore every blessed soul will lose all its vain desires and will have no other desire but to love God and to be loved by Him; and knowing itself secure of always loving God and of being always loved by Him, this will be its blessedness, which will fill it with joy and will make it throughout eternity so satiated with delight that it will desire nothing more.

In a word, this will be the Paradise of the Blessed, to rejoice in the happiness of God. And therefore, he who in this life rejoices in the blessedness which God enjoys, and will enjoy eternally, can say that even in this life he enters into the joy of God and begins to enjoy Paradise.

Meanwhile, O my sweet Saviour and the Love of my soul, I still see myself in this vale of tears surrounded by enemies, who seek to separate me from Thee. O my beloved Lord, permit me not to lose Thee; make me always love Thee, both in this life and in the next, and then dispose of me as Thou pleasest.

O Queen of Paradise, if thou prayest for me, assuredly I shall be with thee eternally, to bear thee company and to praise thee in Paradise.

Reflection 29

The Pain of Having Lost God Is that Which Constitutes Hell

THE grievousness of punishment must correspond to the grievousness of sin. Mortal sin is defined by theologians in a single phrase: "a turning away from God"—turning one's back upon God. And in that consists the malice of mortal sin. It consists in despising the divine grace and in being willing of one's own accord to lose God, the Supreme Good; wherefore, justly the greatest punishment of sinners in Hell is the pain of having lost God.

The other pains of Hell are also great: the devouring fire, the blinding darkness, the deafening shrieks of the damned, the stench which would cause those miserable beings to die (if die they could), the confinement which oppresses and stifles them. But these pains are nothing in comparison to the loss of God. In Hell the reprobate weep eternally, and the bitterest subject of their weeping is the thought that, through their own fault, they have lost God.

And, O God, how great is the good they have lost! In this life, the present objects, the passions, the temporal occupations, the sensible pleasures and the adverse events, hinder us from contemplating the infinite beauty and goodness of God. But when the soul has departed from the prison-house of the body, it does not indeed instantly behold God as He is, for if it saw Him, it would be instantly happy. But it knows that God is an infinite good, infinitely beautiful and worthy of infinite love; hence the soul, which is created to see and love this God, desires to go and unite itself at once with God; but being in sin, it finds an impenetrable wall (which is precisely its sin), which forever closes against it the way which leads to God. O Lord, I thank Thee that this life is not yet ended for me, as I have deserved. I can still come to Thee. "Cast me not away from Thy face." (*Psalms* 50:13). Oh, drive me not away.

The soul, which is created to love its Creator, cannot but find itself impelled by its nature to love its Last End, which is God. In this life, the darkness of sin and earthly affections lull to sleep this inclination which it has to unite itself to God, and therefore it is not greatly afflicted at seeing itself separated from Him; but when it leaves the body and is delivered from the senses, then it sees in clear light that God alone can satisfy it. Hence, as soon as it is set free from the body, immediately it flies to embrace its Supreme Good; but being in sin, it will find itself thrust back by God as an enemy. But though driven away, it will not cease to feel itself ever drawn to unite itself with God; and this will be its hell—to find itself ever drawn toward God and always driven away from God.

Oh, if only the miserable soul which has lost God and can never more see Him could at least find some comfort in loving Him! But no, for having been abandoned by grace and having become the slave of its sin, its will is perverted; hence, on the one side, it will find itself ever drawn to love God, and on the other, it will feel itself constrained to hate Him. Thus, at the same time that it knows that God is worthy of infinite love and praise, it hates Him and curses Him.

Yet perhaps it might in this prison of torments at

least resign itself to the Divine Will, as holy souls do in Purgatory, and bless the hand of that God who justly scourges it. But no, it cannot resign itself because, to do this, the assistance of grace is necessary. But grace (as has been said) has abandoned it; hence, it cannot unite its will to that of God, because its own will is altogether contrary to the Divine Will.

Thus also, it comes to pass that the wretched soul turns all its hatred upon itself and thus will live forever, torn by contrary desires. It would wish to live, it would desire to die. On the one hand, it would live, in order always to hate God, who is the object of its greatest hatred; on the other, it would die, in order not to feel the pain it endures of having lost Him. But it sees that it cannot die. Hence, it will live forever in one continual agony of death. Let us pray God, through the merits of Jesus Christ, to preserve us from Hell; and he especially ought to pray thus who at any time in his life, has lost God through any grievous sin.

O Lord (let him say), save me, and therefore bind me to Thee ever more by Thy holy love; redouble these holy and sweet chains of salvation, that they may ever bind me more firmly to Thee. Wretch that I am, by despising Thy grace I have deserved to be forever separated from Thee, my Sovereign Good, and hate Thee forever! I thank Thee for having borne with me when I was at enmity with Thee; what would have become of me if I had then died? But since Thou hast prolonged my life, grant that I may not use it any more to displease Thee, but only to love Thee, and to weep over the offenses I have committed against Thee. O my Jesus, from this day forth Thou shalt be my only Love, and my only fear shall be no other than that I should offend Thee and separate myself from Thee. But if Thou dost aid me not, I can do nothing; I hope in Thy blood, that Thou wilt give me help to be all

Thine, O my Redeemer, my Love, my All.

O Mary, great advocate of sinners, help a sinner who recommends himself to thee and trusts in thee.

If we would be assured of not losing God, let us give ourselves in earnest wholly to God. *He that does not give himself wholly to God is ever in danger of turning his back upon Him and of losing Him,* but a soul which resolutely detaches itself from everything and gives itself all to God loses Him no more, because God Himself will not allow that a soul which has heartily given itself completely to Him should turn its back upon Him afterwards and perish. Wherefore, a great servant of God was accustomed to say that, when we read of the fall of certain persons who had before given tokens of living a holy life, we must conclude that such persons had not given themselves completely to God.

Reflection 30

On Contempt of the World

THE thought of the vanity of the world and that all the things which the world values are but falsehood and deceit has made many souls resolve to give themselves wholly to God. "What doth it profit a man, if he gain the whole world, and suffer the loss of his own soul?" (*Matthew* 16:26). How many young persons has this great maxim of the Gospel brought to leave relations, country, possessions, honors and even crowns, to go and shut themselves up in a cloister or desert, there to think of God alone! The day of death is called the day of loss or destruction. "The day of destruction is at hand." (*Deuteronomy* 32:35). It is a day of loss, because all the goods which we have acquired on earth must all be left on the day of our death. Wherefore, St. Ambrose wisely says that we falsely call these goods our own goods because we cannot carry them with us into the other world, where we must dwell forever. It is our good works alone which accompany us, and they alone will console us in eternity.

All earthly fortunes, the highest dignities, gold, silver, the most precious jewels, when looked at from the bed of death, lose their splendor; the fatal shadow of death obscures even scepters and crowns and makes us see that all which the world values is but smoke, dust, vanity and misery. And in truth, at the time of

death, what use is there for all the riches acquired
by one who is dying, if nothing belongs to him after
death, except a wooden box in which he is placed to
rot? What will the boasted beauty of the body serve
when there remains of it only a little fetid dust and
a few fleshless bones?

What is the life of man upon earth? Behold it as
described by St. James: "What is your life? It is a vapor
which appeareth for a little while, and afterwards shall
vanish away." (*James* 4:15). Today this great man is
esteemed, feared, praised; tomorrow he is despised,
slandered, and cursed. "I have seen the wicked highly
exalted . . ." says the Psalmist, "and I passed by, and
lo he was not." (*Psalms* 36:35-36). He is no longer to
be found in this his beloved villa, in this grand palace
which he built himself; and where is he? He is become
dust in the grave!

"There is a deceitful balance in his hand." (*Osee*
12:7). In these words the Holy Spirit warns us not to
be deceived by the world, because the world weighs its
goods in a false balance. We ought to weigh things in
the true balance of faith, which will show us what are
true goods, which those things can never be called that
soon perish. St. Teresa used to say: "We should not
take account of anything which ends with death." O
God, what has there remained of greatness to so many
first ministers of state, to so many commanders of
armies, to so many princes, to so many Roman emperors—now that for them the scene is changed, and they
find themselves in eternity? "Their memory has per-
ished with a noise." (*Psalms* 9:7). They made a great
figure in the world, and their names resounded every-
where; but after they were dead, rank, name and everything was ended for them. It is useful to record here
an inscription placed over a certain cemetery in which
many men and women of rank are buried:

"Behold the end of all the pomp of earth, All human greatness, beauty, noble birth! Worms, rottenness, a little dust, a stone, Close the brief scene of life for ev'ry one."

"The fashion of this world passeth away." (*1 Corinthians* 7:31). Our life, finally, is but a scene which passes away and speedily ends; and it must end for all, whether nobles or commoners, kings or subjects, rich or poor. Happy is he who in this scene has played his part well before God. Philip III, king of Spain, died young, at the age of forty-two years; and before he died, he said to those around him: "When I am dead, proclaim the spectacle which you now see; proclaim that, in death, to have been a king serves only to make one feel regret of having reigned." And then he ended with a sigh, saying: "Oh, that during this time I had been in a desert, becoming a saint; for now I should appear with more confidence before the tribunal of Jesus Christ!"

We know the change of life which St. Francis Borgia made at the sight of the corpse of the Empress Isabella, who in life was most beautiful, but after death, struck horror in all who saw her. On beholding her, he exclaimed: "Such then is the end of all the grandeur of this world!" And he gave himself wholly to God. Oh, that we would all imitate him before death comes upon us! But let us make haste, because death runs towards us, and we know not when it will arrive. Let us not so act that nothing will remain of the light which God now gives us but remorse, and the account to be rendered of it to God, when we hold in our hands the candle at death. Let us resolve to do now what then we shall wish to have done and shall no longer be able to do.

No, my God, Thou hast borne with me long enough! I do not wish to make Thee wait any longer before seeing me give myself wholly to Thee. Thou hast many times called me to have done with the world and to give myself competely to Thy love. Now Thou callest me again! Behold me, receive me into Thy arms, for at this moment I abandon myself wholly to Thee. O spotless Lamb, who didst once sacrifice Thyself on Calvary, dying on a cross for me, first wash me with Thy blood and pardon all the injuries Thou hast received from me, and then inflame me with Thy holy love. I love Thee above everything; I love Thee with all my soul. And what object can I find in the world more worthy of love than Thou art, or one who has loved me more?

O Mary, Mother of God, and my Advocate, pray to Him for me; obtain for me a true and lasting change of life. In thee I trust.

Reflection 31

On the Love of Solitude

GOD does not allow Himself to be found in the tumult of the world; therefore, the Saints were accustomed to seek the most frightful deserts, the most hidden caves, in order that they might flee from men and converse with God alone. St. Hilarion made trial of several deserts, going from one to another, ever seeking the most solitary one, where there should be no man with whom to speak. And in the end, he died in a desert of Cyprus, after having lived there for five years. St. Bruno, when he was called by God to leave the world, went with his companions who wished to follow him, to find St. Hugh, Bishop of Grenoble, that he might assign them some desert place in his diocese. St. Hugh assigned them the Carthusian mountains, which from their frightful wildness, were more fitted to be a resort of wild beasts than a habitation for men; and there they went with joy to dwell, each living in a little hut at a distance from the rest.

Our Lord said once to St. Teresa: "I would willingly speak to many souls, but the world makes so much noise in their hearts that My voice cannot be heard." God does not speak to us in the midst of the tumult and business of the world, knowing that if He speaks, He is not heard. The words of God are His holy inspirations, His lights and calls, by which the Saints are enlightened and inflamed with divine love; but he who does not love solitude will not be allowed to hear these voices of God.

God Himself declares: "I . . . will lead her into the wilderness, and I will speak to her heart." (*Osee* 2:14). When God desires to raise anyone to a high degree of perfection, He induces him to retire to some solitary place, far from the converse of creatures, and there He speaks to the ears—not of the body, but of the heart—and thus He enlightens and inflames him with His divine love.

St. Bernard used to say that he had learned much more of the love of God among the oaks and beeches of the forest than from books and from the servants of God. Therefore, St. Jerome left the pleasures of Rome and shut himself up in the cave of Bethlehem, and afterwards exclaimed: "O solitude, in which God speaks familiarly and converses with His own!" In solitude God converses familiarly with His beloved souls, and there He makes them hear those words which melt their hearts with holy love, as the sacred Spouse said: "My soul melted when he [my Beloved] spoke." (*Canticle of Canticles* 5:6).

We see by experience that treating with the world and occupying ourselves in the acquisition of earthly goods makes us forget God; but at the hour of death, what shall we find of all the labor and time we have spent upon the things of earth, except affliction and remorse of conscience? At death we shall find comfort only from that little which we have done and suffered for God. Why, then, do we not detach ourselves from the world before death separates it from us?

"He shall sit solitary, and hold his peace because he hath taken it up upon himself." (*Lamentations* 3:28). The solitary is not engaged as he formerly was in worldly affairs; he will sit in repose, and he will hold his peace and will not call for sensual delights to satisfy him because, lifted up above himself and above all created things, he will find in God every good and all his happiness.

"Who will give me wings like a dove, and I will fly and be at rest?" (*Psalms* 54:7). David desired to have the wings of a dove, that he might leave this earth and not touch it even with his feet, and thus give rest to his soul. But so long as we are in this life, it is not given to us to leave this earth; let us at least take care to love retirement, so far as it is practicable, conversing alone with God, and thus gain strength to avoid defects in our unavoidable intercourse with the world, as David did at the very time he was ruling his kingdom: "Lo," he says, "I have gone far off, flying away, and I abode in the wilderness." (*Psalms* 54:8).

Oh, that I had always thought of Thee, O God of my soul, and not of the goods of this world! I curse those days in which, seeking pleasures, I have offended Thee, my Sovereign Good. Oh that I had always loved Thee! Oh that I had died and not caused Thee displeasure! Miserable that I am, death draws near while I find myself still attached to the world! No, my Jesus, this day I resolve to leave all and to be entirely Thine. Thou art almighty, Thou hast to give me strength to be faithful to Thee.

O Mother of God, pray to Jesus for me!

Reflection 32

On Solitude of Heart

SAINT GREGORY wrote: "What does the solitude of the body profit if the solitude of the heart is not there?" In the preceding reflection we have seen how much solitude assists recollection of mind, but St. Gregory says that it profits us little or nothing to be with the body in a solitary place, while we still keep the heart full of worldly thoughts and affections. That a soul may be wholly given to God, two things are necessary: the first is to detach one's self from the love of every created thing; the second is to consecrate all one's love to God. And this is what true solitude of heart means.

We must in the first place, then, detach our hearts from every earthly affection. St. Francis de Sales used to say: "If I knew that I had a single fiber in my heart which was not given to God, I would instantly pluck it out." If we do not purify and strip the heart of everything earthly, the love of God cannot enter in and possess it entirely. God would reign by His love in our hearts, but He would reign there alone; He will have no companions to rob Him of a portion of that affection which He justly claims to have entirely for Himself.

Some souls complain that in all their devout exercises, meditations, Communions, spiritual readings, visits to the Blessed Sacrament, they do not find God and

112

know not what means to adopt in order to find Him. St. Teresa gives them the right means when she says: "Detach thy heart from all created things, and then seek God, and thou shalt find Him."

Many persons cannot, in order to separate themselves from creatures and converse with God alone, go and live in a desert, as they would wish; but we must understand that deserts and caves are not necessary in order to enjoy solitude of heart. Those who from necessity are obliged to converse with the world—provided that their hearts are free from worldly attachments—can, even in the streets, in places of resort and in public assemblies, possess solitude of heart and remain united with God. All those occupations which are undertaken to fulfill the Divine Will do not prevent the solitude of the heart. St. Catherine of Siena was able to find God in the midst of the household labors in which her parents kept her employed in order to withdraw her from devotional exercises; but in the midst of these affairs she remained retired within her heart, which she called her cell, and there ceased not to converse alone with God.

"Be still and see that I am God," says the Psalmist. (*Psalms* 45:11). To possess that divine light which enables us to know the goodness of God, which when known, is well able to draw to itself all the affections of our heart, we must be still, that is, disentangle ourselves from the earthly attachments which hinder us from knowing God. As a crystal vase when it is filled with sand cannot receive the light of the sun, so a heart which is attached to riches, to worldly honors, or to sensual pleasures, cannot receive the divine light; and not knowing God, it does not love Him. In every state in which a man finds himself placed by God, he must indeed give attention to perform his duties according to the pleasure of God; but to prevent creatures

from drawing him away from God, he must in everything else act as if there were no one else in the world
except himself and God.

We must detach ourselves from everything, and especially from ourselves, by continually thwarting our self-
love. For example, a certain thing pleases us; we must
leave it for the very reason that it pleases us. A certain person has injured us; we must do him good just
because he has injured us. In a word, we must will
and not will, exactly as God wills or does not will,
without wishing for anything whatever until we know
that it is the will of God that we should desire it.

Oh, how easily does God let Himself be found by
everyone who detaches himself from creatures in order
to find Him! "The Lord is good . . . to the soul that
seeketh Him." (*Lamentations* 3:25). St. Francis de Sales
says: "The pure love of God consumes everything which
is not God, in order to convert everything into itself."
We must therefore make ourselves an enclosed garden, as the holy spouse in the *Canticles* is called by
God. "My sister, my spouse, is a garden enclosed." (*Canticle of Canticles* 4:12). The soul which keeps the door
shut against earthly affections is called an enclosed
garden. God has given us everything that we have,
and it is reasonable that He should require of us all
our love. When, then, any creature would enter and
take for itself a portion of our love, we must altogether
deny it any entrance, and turning to our Sovereign
Good, we must say with all our affection: "What have
I in Heaven? And besides Thee what do I desire on
earth? . . . Thou art the God of my heart, and the God
that is my portion forever." (*Psalms* 72:25-26). "O my
God, what but Thyself can satisfy my soul? No, I desire
nothing but Thee, either in Heaven or on earth; Thou
alone art sufficient for me, O God of my heart and my
Portion forever."

Oh, happy is he who can say: "The kingdom of the earth and all worldly pomp I have despised for the love of my Lord Jesus Christ." Truly, that great servant of God, sister Margaret of the Cross, the daughter of the Emperor Maximilian II, could say this when at her profession she stripped herself of her rich garments and jewels to clothe herself in the poor woolen habit of the barefooted nuns of the strict rule of St. Clare and when, as the author of her life relates, she cast them away with a contempt which moved to tears of devotion all who assisted at the function.

O my Jesus, for my part I do not desire that creatures should have any share in my heart; Thou must be its only Lord, by possessing it entirely. Let others seek the delights and grandeurs of this earth; Thou alone, both in the present and the future life, must be my only Portion, my only Good, my only Love. And, since Thou hast loved me, as I see by the proofs Thou givest me, help me to detach myself from everything which can divert me from Thy love. Grant that my soul may be entirely taken up with pleasing Thee, as the only object of all my affections. Take possession of all my heart; I will be no longer my own. Do Thou rule me and make me prompt to execute Thy will.

O Mary, Mother of God, in thee I trust; thy prayers have to make me belong wholly to Jesus.

Reflection 33

To See and Love God in the Next Life Is the Joy of the Blessed in Paradise

LET us see what it is in Heaven that makes those holy citizens completely happy. The soul in Heaven, seeing God face to face and knowing His infinite beauty and all His perfections, which render Him worthy of infinite love, cannot but love Him with all its powers, and loves Him far more than itself. Nay, even forgetting itself, as it were, it thinks of nothing and desires nothing but to see Him happy who is its Beloved and its God; and seeing that God, the only Object of all its affections, enjoys an infinite happiness, this happiness of God constitutes its entire Paradise. If a soul were capable of anything infinite, its own joy would also be infinite in seeing that its Beloved is infinitely happy; but as a creature is not capable of infinite joy, the soul is at least satiated with joy, so that it desires nothing more. And this is that happiness for which David sighed when he said: "I shall be satisfied when Thy glory shall appear." (*Psalms* 16:15).

Thus is fulfilled what God says to the soul when He puts it in possession of Paradise: "Enter thou into the joy of thy Lord." (*Matthew* 25:21). He does not bid the joy enter into the soul, because this His joy, being infinite, cannot be contained in the creature; but He bids

116

the soul enter into *His* joy, that it may receive a portion of it, and a portion so great as to satiate it and fill it with delight.

Therefore, I think that in prayer, among all the acts of love for God, there is no act of love more perfect than taking delight in the infinite happiness which God enjoys. This is certainly the continual exercise of the Blessed in Heaven; so that he who often rejoices in the happiness of God begins in this life to do that which he hopes to do in Heaven through all eternity.

The love for God with which the Saints in Paradise burn is so great that, if a fear of losing Him or of not loving Him with all their powers (as now they love Him) should ever enter their minds, this fear would cause them to experience a very hell of anguish. But no, for they are as sure as they are sure of God that they will love Him always with all their powers and that they will be ever loved by God, and that this mutual love will never change throughout eternity. O my God, make me worthy of this certainty through the merits of Jesus Christ.

This happiness which constitutes Paradise, moreover will be increased by the splendor of that delightful City of God, by the beauty of its inhabitants and by their companionship, especially by that of the Queen of all, Mary, who will appear fairer than all, and by that of Jesus Christ, whose beauty again will immensely surpass that of Mary.

The joy of the Blessed will be increased by the knowledge of the dangers of losing so great a Good which each one has passed through in this life. What, then, will be the thanksgiving offered to God by one who had unhappily deserved Hell by his sins and now finds himself there on high, whence he will see so many condemned to Hell for less sins than his own, while he is saved and sure of not losing God, destined to enjoy eternally in Heaven those boundless delights of which he will never grow weary! In this life, however great and continual be our joys, in time they weary us; but as for the delights of Paradise, the more they are enjoyed, the more they are desired, so that the Blessed are always fully satisfied with these delights and always desire them; they ever desire them and ever obtain them. Wherefore, that sweet song with which the Saints praise God and thank Him for the happiness He has given them is called a new canticle: "Sing ye to the Lord a new canticle." (*Psalms* 97:1). It is called new because the joys of Heaven seem ever as new as when they were tasted the first time, because they always possess them yet always long for them; they ever desire them and ever experience them. Thus, as the damned are called "vessels of wrath," the Blessed are called "vessels of divine love."

Justly, then, does St. Augustine say that, to gain this eternal blessedness, there ought to be eternal labor. Hence, it was little that the anchorites did with their penitential works and prayers to gain Paradise; it was little for the Saints to leave their riches and kingdoms to gain Paradise; little that so many martyrs suffered in enduring racks and burning irons and cruel deaths to gain Paradise.

Let us at least take care to suffer joyfully the crosses which God sends us, because all of them, if we are saved, will procure for us eternal joys. When infirmities, pains or other adversities afflict us, let us lift up our eyes to Heaven and say: "One day all these pains will have an end, and after that I hope to enjoy God forever." Let us take courage to suffer and to despise all the things of the world. Blessed is he who at death will be able to say with St. Agatha: "O Lord, who hast taken from me the love of the world, receive my soul." Let us endure everything, let us despise all that is created; Jesus awaits us and stands with the crown in His hands to make us kings in Heaven, if we be faithful to Him.

But how can I, O my Jesus, aspire to so great a good, I, who have so often for the sake of the miserable pleasures of earth renounced Paradise before Thy face and have trodden underfoot Thy grace? Yet Thy blood gives me courage to hope for Paradise, though I have so often deserved Hell. Yes, I hope for it because Thou hast died upon the Cross precisely in order to bestow Paradise upon those who have not deserved it. O my Redeemer and my God, I resolve to lose Thee no more; do Thou give me help to be faithful to Thee; Thy Kingdom come; through the merits of Thy blood, grant me one day to enter Thy Kingdom; and in the meantime, until death shall come, enable me to fulfill Thy will perfectly, which is the greatest good and is a paradise such as can be possessed upon earth by him who loves Thee.

Therefore, O ye souls who love God, while we live in this vale of tears, let us ever sigh for Paradise and say:

> "O beauteous home! where love's reward
>   Love will itself bestow;
> Where my so sweet and loving Lord
>   Himself unveiled will show;
> When shall I see that blest abode,
>   And there behold and love my God?
> When will that wished-for dawn arise?
>   While now I cry, 'twixt smiles and tears,
> Ah, when? Ah, when shall end my fears?
>   O Paradise! O Paradise!"

On Prayer before the Most Holy Sacrament of the Altar

MEDITATION, wherever it is made, pleases God; but it seems that Jesus Christ especially delights in the prayer which is made before the Most Holy Sacrament, since it appears that there He bestows light and grace more abundantly upon those who visit Him. He has left Himself in this Sacrament, not only to be the food of the souls who receive Him in Holy Communion, but also to be found present at all times by everyone who seeks Him. Devout pilgrims go to the holy house of Loreto, where Jesus Christ dwelt during His life, and to Jerusalem, where He died on the Cross; but how much greater ought to be our devotion when we find ourselves before a tabernacle, where this Lord Himself now dwells in person, who once lived among us and died for us on Calvary!

It is not permitted here on earth for persons of all ranks to speak alone with kings; but with Jesus Christ, the King of Heaven, all—both noble and plebeians, rich and poor—can converse at will in this Sacrament and remain as long as they will to lay before Him their needs and to seek His graces. And there Jesus gives audience to all, and hears and comforts all.

Men of the world, who know no pleasures but those of earth, cannot comprehend what pleasure can be found in spending a long time before an altar, where there is a consecrated Host. But to souls who love God, hours and days passed before the Blessed Sacrament seem but moments because of the heavenly sweetness which Our Lord there makes them taste and enjoy.

But how can worldly people expect to enjoy these sweetnesses if they keep their hearts and minds full of the earth? St. Francis Borgia used to say that in order that divine love may rule in our hearts, we must first banish from them the world; otherwise, divine love will never enter into them, because it finds no place to rest: "Be still, and see that I am God," said David. (*Psalms* 45:11). In order to have a relish for God and to taste how sweet He is to them that love Him, our hearts must be empty, that is, detached from earthly affections. Wouldst thou find God? "Detach thyself from creatures, and thou shalt find Him," says St. Teresa.

What should a soul do when in the presence of the Blessed Sacrament? It should love and pray. It should not stay there in order to experience sweetnesses and consolations, but only to give pleasure to God by making acts of love, by giving itself wholly to God without reserve, by stripping itself of all self-will and by offering itself, saying: "O my God, I love Thee and desire nothing but Thee; grant that I may always love Thee, and then do with me and with all that I possess whatever Thou pleasest." Among all acts of love, the most agreeable to God is that which the Blessed continually exercise in Heaven, that is to say, rejoicing in the infinite happiness which God enjoys. For, as we have already said, the soul in Heaven loves God immeasurably more than itself and therefore desires the happiness of its Beloved far more than its own; and seeing that God enjoys an infinite happiness, it would thereby feel an infinite delight; but as a creature is not capable of an infinite delight, it is at least quite filled with joy, so that the happiness of God constitutes its joy and its Paradise. These acts of love, even when made by us without any sensible sweetness, please God greatly. For the rest, God gives to His most beloved souls the enjoyment of His consolations in this life, not always, but only rarely; and when He does give them, He gives them, not so much as a reward for their good works (the full recompense of which He reserves for them in Heaven), as to give them more courage to suffer with patience the troubles and adversities of this present life and especially to bear with the distractions and dryness which pious souls experience in prayer.

As for distractions, of these we must not make any account; it is enough to drive them away when we perceive them. For the rest, even Saints suffer involuntary distractions, but they do not on this account leave off prayer. Neither must we do so ourselves. St. Francis de Sales said that, if in meditation we did nothing but drive away distractions again and again, our meditation would nevertheless be of great profit. Then, as for dryness, the greatest pain of souls given to prayer is to find themselves sometimes without any feeling of devotion, weary of it and without any sensible [i.e., "perceived"] desire of loving God; and with this is often joined the fear of being under God's displeasure on account of their sins, for which He may have abandoned them; and being in this utter darkness, they know not any way of escaping from it, for it seems to them that every way is closed against them. Let the devout soul, then, continue firm not to leave off meditation, as the devil intends. At such times, let the soul unite its desolation with that which Jesus Christ suffered upon the Cross; and if it can say nothing else, it is enough to say this, at least by an act of the will: "My God, I desire to love Thee; I wish to be wholly Thine. Have pity on me; abandon me not!" Say also, as a holy soul used to say to God in a time of greatest desolation:

> "I love Thee, though I seem to be
> But hateful in Thy sight;
> And I will ever follow Thee
> Where'er Thou turn Thy flight."

In God Alone True Peace Is Found

HE that seeks peace in creatures will never find it, because no creatures are capable of giving contentment to the heart. God has created man for Himself, who is an infinite good; therefore, God alone can satisfy him. Hence it comes that many persons, though loaded with riches, honors and earthly pleasures, are never satisfied; they are ever yearning for more honors, more possessions, more amusements; and however many they obtain, they are always restless and never enjoy a day of true peace. "Delight in the Lord, and He will give thee the requests of thy heart." (*Psalms* 36:4). When any person delights only in God and seeks nothing but God, God Himself will take care to satisfy all the desires of his heart; and then he will attain the happy state of those souls who desire nothing but to please God.

Senseless are they who say: "Happy is he who can employ himself as he likes, who can command others, who can take what pleasure he pleases." It is madness; he alone is happy who loves God, who says that God alone is sufficient for him. Experience shows clearly that so many persons called fortunate by men of the world, however much they are raised up to the possession of great riches and great dignities, lead an unhappy life and never find rest.

But how is this that so many persons, rich and titled, and even princes, in the midst of the abundance of the goods of the world, do not find peace? And, on the contrary, so many good religious, who live retired in a cell, poor and hidden, live so contentedly? How was it that so many solitaries, living in a desert or in a cave, suffering hunger and cold, yet exulted with joy? It is because they lived for God alone, and God consoled them.

"The peace of God . . . surpasseth all understanding." (*Philippians* 4:7). Oh, how much does not the peace which the Lord gives to those who love Him exceed all the delights which the world can give! "O taste and see that the Lord is sweet!" (*Psalms* 33:9). O men of the world, cries the prophet, why will ye despise the life of the Saints, without having ever known it? Try it for once; leave the world, leave it and give yourselves to God, and you shall see how well He knows how to console you more than can all the grandeurs and delights of the world.

It is true that even the Saints suffer great trials in this life; but they, resigning themselves to the Will of God, never lose their peace. The lovers of the world are seen to be at times joyful and at times sad, but in truth they are ever restless and in trouble. On the contrary, the lovers of God are superior to all adversities and to the changes of this world, and therefore they always live in uniform tranquility. See how the celebrated Cardinal Petrucci describes a soul wholly given to God: "It beholds creatures around it changing into various forms, while within the depths of its heart, it lives ever united to God without change."

But he who would be always united with God and would enjoy a continual peace must drive from his heart everything which is not God and live as one dead to earthly affections. O my God, give me help to disengage myself from all the snares which draw me to the world. Grant that I may think of nothing but pleasing Thee.

Happy are they for whom God alone is sufficient!

O Lord, give me grace that I may seek nothing but Thee and desire nothing but to love Thee and give Thee pleasure. For love of Thee I now renounce all earthly pleasure. I renounce also all spiritual consolations. I desire nothing but to do Thy will and to give Thee pleasure.

O Mother of God, recommend me to thy Son, who denies thee nothing.

Reflection 36

We Ought to Have God Alone in View

IN ALL our actions we should have no other end in view but to please God, not to please our relations or friends or great people or ourselves, because everything which is not done for the sake of God is all lost. Many things are done to please or not to displease men, but says St. Paul: "If I yet pleased men, I should not be the servant of Christ." (*Galatians* 1:10). God only must be regarded in everything we do, so that we may say as Jesus Christ said: "I do always the things that please Him." (*John* 8:29). God has given us everything we have; we have of our own only nothingness and sin. God alone is He who has truly loved us. He has loved us from eternity, and He has loved us even so as to give Himself to us upon the Cross and in the Sacrament of the Altar. God alone, therefore, deserves all our love.

Unhappy is that soul which looks with affection upon any object upon earth to the displeasure of God. It will never know peace in this life and is in imminent peril of never enjoying peace in the next. But on the contrary, happy is he, O my God, who seeks Thee alone and renounces everything for Thy love! He will find that pearl of Thy pure love, a jewel more precious than all the treasures and kingdoms of the earth. He that does this, obtains the true liberty of the sons of God, for he finds himself freed from all the bonds which draw him to earth and hinder him from uniting himself closely to God.

My God and my All, I prefer Thee to all riches, to honors, to knowledge, to glory, to expectations and to all the gifts which Thou couldst bestow on me. Thou art entirely my Good; Thee alone I desire and nothing more, for Thou alone art infinitely beautiful, infinitely kind, infinitely amiable; in a word, Thou art the Only Good. Wherefore, every gift which is not Thyself is not enough for me. I repeat, and I will ever repeat it, Thee alone I desire and nothing more; and whatever is less than Thee, I tell Thee, it is not sufficient for me.

Oh, when shall it be given me to occupy myself solely in praising Thee, loving Thee and pleasing Thee, so that I shall no more think of creatures, nor even of myself? O my Lord and my Love, help me when Thou seest me growing cold in Thy love, in danger of giving my affection to creatures and to earthly pleasures. "Put forth Thy hand from on high, take me out, and deliver me from many waters." (*Psalms* 143:7). Deliver me at that time from the danger of going far away from Thee.

Let others seek what they will; nothing pleases me and I desire nothing but Thee, my God, my Love and my Hope: "What have I in Heaven? And besides Thee, what do I desire upon earth? . . . Thou art the God of my heart, and the God that is my portion forever." (*Psalms* 75:25-26). My God and my all!

O men, let us undeceive ourselves! All the good which comes to us from creatures is but dust, smoke and deceits; God alone is He who can satisfy us. But in this life He does not grant us to enjoy Him fully; He only gives us certain foretastes of the good things which He promises in Heaven. There He awaits us to satiate us with His own bliss, when He will say to us: "Enter thou into the joy of thy Lord." (*Matthew* 25:21). The Lord gives heavenly consolations to His servants, only to make them yearn for that happiness which He prepares for them in Paradise.

O Almighty God, O God worthy of love, grant that in all things from henceforth we may aim at nothing and seek nothing but Thy pleasure. Grant that Thou mayest be our All and our only Love, since Thou alone, both in justice and in gratitude, dost deserve all our affections. Nothing gives me greater pain than the thought that in times past I have so little loved Thine Infinite Goodness, but I desire and resolve, with Thy help, to love Thee with all my strength for the time to come, and thus I hope to die, loving Thee alone, my Sovereign Good.

O Mary, Mother of God, pray for me, a miserable creature. Thy prayers are never refused; pray to Jesus that He may make me entirely His own.

Reflection 37

Everything Should Be Endured to Please God

THIS has been the one only and dearest endeavor of all the Saints, to desire with their whole heart to endure every toil, all contempt, every pain, in order to give pleasure to God and thus to please that Divine Heart which so much deserves to be loved and loves us so much.

In this consists all perfection and the love of a soul for God—in its always seeking the pleasure of God and doing that which most pleases God. Oh blessed is he who can say with Jesus Christ: "I do always the things that please Him!" (*John* 8:29). And what greater honor, what greater consolation can a soul have than to go through some fatigue or to accept some affliction with the thought of giving pleasure to God? Too great is our obligation to give pleasure to that God who has loved us so much, who has given us all that we possess and who, not content with giving us so many good things, has gone so far as to give Himself to us, first on the Cross, dying upon it for love of us, and afterwards in the Sacrament of the Altar, where He gives Himself entirely to us in Holy Communion, so that He has nothing more that He can give us.

On this account, the Saints knew not what more they could do in order to give pleasure to God. How many young nobles have left the world in order to give themselves wholly to God! How many young maidens, even of royal blood, have renounced marriage with the great in order to shut themselves up in a cloister! How many anchorites have gone to hide themselves in deserts and caves in order to meditate upon God alone! How many martyrs have embraced scourges and red-hot iron plates and the most cruel torments of tyrants in order to please God! In a word, in order to give pleasure to God, the Saints have stripped themselves of their possessions, have renounced the greatest earthly dignities and have accepted as treasures, infirmities, persecutions, the loss of their goods and a death the most painful and desolate.

The good pleasure of God, therefore, if we truly love it, ought to be preferred by us to the acquisition of all the riches, of all the honors, of all the delights of earth, and even of Paradise itself. Yes, for it is certain that all the Blessed, if they were to know that it would please God more that they should burn in Hell, one and all, even the Mother of God, would cast themselves into that abyss of fire and suffer eternally in order to give greater pleasure to God.

For this end has God placed us in the world, in order that we may labor to please Him and give Him glory. Wherefore, to give satisfaction to God ought to be the one object of all our desires, of all our thoughts and actions. Well does that Heart deserve to be pleased in all things which has so greatly loved us and is so anxious for our good.

But how is it, O Lord, that I, an ungrateful wretch, instead of seeking to give Thee pleasure, have so often displeased Thee? Yet the detestation which Thou makest me feel for the sins I have committed against Thee causes me to hope that Thou art willing to pardon me.

Pardon me, then, and suffer me not to be ungrateful to Thee any more. Grant that I may overcome everything to give Thee pleasure. "In Thee, O Lord, have I hoped; I shall not be confounded forever." (*Psalms* 30:1).

O Queen of Heaven and my mother, draw me entirely to God.

Reflection 38

Blessed Is He who Desires Nothing but God

"BLESSED are the poor in spirit, for theirs is the Kingdom of Heaven." (*Matthew* 5:3). By "the poor in spirit" are meant those who are poor in earthly desires, and wish for nothing but God. These are poor in affection, but not in reality, since they live contented, even in this life; and therefore Our Lord does not say: "Theirs shall be the kingdom of heaven," but "theirs *is*," because even in this life they are rich in spiritual goods which they receive from God. Thus, however poor they are in temporal goods, they live content with their condition. They are different from those who are rich in earthly desires, who in the present life, whatever riches they possess, are always poor and live discontented. For the good things of this life do not satisfy our thirst, however much they are increased; wherefore, these persons are never contented, never attaining to the acquisition of as much as they desire.

In order to enrich us with true riches, Jesus Christ chose to be poor, as the Apostle writes: "He became poor for your sakes, that through His poverty you might be rich." (*2 Corinthians* 8:9). He chose to be poor, in order to teach us by His example to despise earthly goods and thus to make us rich with heavenly goods,

133

which are immensely more precious and are eternal. Therefore, He declared that whoever did not renounce everything on earth that he possesses with attachment could not be His true follower.

Happy is he who desires nothing but God and says with St. Paulinus: "Let the rich have their riches and kings their kingdoms; Christ is my riches and my kingdom." Let us persuade ourselves that God alone can content us, but He does not fully content any but those souls that love Him with all their hearts. And what room can the love of God find in a heart that is full of this earth? Such people may go often to Communion and pay frequent visits to the Blessed Sacrament, but because this love of earth is in their hearts, God cannot wholly possess them and enrich them as He would.

Many souls lament that in their meditations and Communions and in their other most devout exercises they do not find God. To such, St. Teresa says: "Detach thy heart from creatures, and thou shalt find God." Let us strip ourselves of every affection which is of earth, and especially of our own will. Let us give to God our whole will without reserve and say to Him: "Lord, do Thou dispose of me and of all I have as Thou pleasest; I desire nothing but what Thou desirest, and I know that what Thou willest is best for me. Grant me, then, that I may ever love Thee, and I desire nothing more."

Now, the only means to detach ourselves from creatures is to acquire a great love for God. If the love of God does not succeed in obtaining the mastery over our whole will, we shall never succeed in becoming saints. The means for acquiring this all-holy love is prayer. Let us constantly pray to God to give us His love, for thus we shall find ourselves detached from everything created. Divine love is a thief, which in a holy way robs us of all earthly affections and causes us to say: "What else do I desire but Thee alone, O God of my heart!"

"Love is strong as death." (*Canticle of Canticles* 8:6). This means, that as there is no power which resists death, so there is nothing, even of things most difficult to overcome, which can resist divine love. Love conquers all. By the love of God the holy martyrs conquered the fiercest torments, and the most painful deaths.

Oh happy, in a word, is he who can say with David: "What have I in Heaven? And besides Thee, what do I desire upon earth? . . . Thou art the God of my heart, and the God that is my portion forever!" (*Psalms* 72:25-26). What else can I desire in this life and in eternity but Thee alone, O my God? Let others have the good things they desire; be Thou, O God of my heart, my only Good; be Thou all my Peace.

Alas, the soul is always in danger of abandoning God and being lost, so long as it has not given itself wholly to God; while he who has truly given himself entirely to God can rest secure of never leaving Him, because Our Lord is indeed kind and faithful to everyone who has given himself to Him without reserve. But why is it that some persons who at first lived a holy life afterwards fell so grievously that they left little hope of their salvation? Why is this? Because, I answer, they had not given themselves wholly to God, and this their fall is the proof of it.

O my God, and my true Lover, suffer not that my soul, which was created to love Thee, should love anything apart from Thee and should not wholly belong to Thee, who hast purchased me with Thy blood. O my Jesus, how is it possible that, after having known the love which Thou hast borne me, I can love any object besides Thee? Draw me always more within Thy heart;

make me forget everything, so that I may not seek nor sigh after anything but Thy love. O my Jesus, in Thee I trust.

O Mary, Mother of God, in thee are my hopes; detach me from the love of everything which is not God, that He may be the object of all my affections and of my eternal happiness.

Reflection 39

On Dryness of Spirit

SAINT FRANCIS de Sales says that true devotion and the true love of God do not consist in feeling spiritual consolations in prayer and other devout exercises, but in having a resolute will to do and to will nothing but what God wills. This is the one end for which we should apply ourselves to prayer, to Communion, to mortification and to every other thing which is pleasing to God, although we do them without relish and in the midst of a thousand temptations and in weariness of spirit. "With aridity and temptations," says St. Teresa, "God makes trial of those who love Him. Even if the whole life should be passed in dryness, let not the soul leave off prayer; the time will come when all will be abundantly rewarded."

As the masters of the spiritual life recommend, in a time of desolation we ought principally to exercise ourselves in acts of humility and resignation. There is no better time for learning our own helplessness and our misery than when we are dry in prayer, wearied, distracted and disgusted, without any sensible fervor, and even without any apparent desires of making progress in divine love. At such times let the soul say: "Lord, have mercy upon me; behold how powerless I am to make even a good act!" Besides, we must resign ourselves and say: "O my God, is it Thy will to keep me thus in darkness, thus in affliction? May Thy holy will be ever done. I desire not to be consoled; it is enough for me to remain here, solely to give Thee pleasure." And thus we ought to persevere in our prayer during the appointed time.

The greatest pain, however, which a soul given to prayer suffers is not so much dryness, as a darkness in which it finds itself stripped of all good will, and tempted against Faith and against Hope. Sometimes, in addition, it experiences violent attacks of temptations and such distrust that it is in grievous fear of having lost even the grace of God; and it seems to it, as if on account of its sins, God had already driven it away from Him and had abandoned it, so that in this state, the soul looks upon itself as if hated by God; and therefore, at such times even solitude torments it, and mental prayer seems to it a kind of hell. Then must it take courage, and it must know that these fears of having yielded to temptation or to despair are indeed fears and the torment of the soul, but not voluntary acts and therefore are free from sin. At such a time a person really resists temptation with his will, though on account of the darkness which bewilders him, he is not able distinctly to perceive it. And this is proved by experience, for if afterwards he were to be tempted to commit knowingly a simple venial sin, his soul, which loves God, would rather accept death a thousand times.

On this account, we must not trouble ourselves at such times to attain a certainty that we are in the grace of God and that there was no sin. You then want to know and to be sure that God loves you, but at this time God does not choose to let you know it. He wills that you should only strive to humble yourself and trust in His Goodness and resign yourself to His Will. You want to see, and God does not will that you should see. For the rest, St. Francis de Sales says that the resolution which you have (at least in your will) to love God and not to give Him deliberately the least displeasure is an assurance that you are in the grace of God. Abandon yourself, therefore, at such times into the arms of the Divine Mercy; protest to God that you desire nothing but Him and His Will, and fear not. Oh, how dear to Almighty God are these acts of confidence and resignation made in the midst of this terrible darkness!

For forty-one years St. Jane Frances de Chantal suffered these interior pains, accompanied by horrible temptations and by fears that she was in a state of sin and was abandoned by God. So great was her anguish that she used to say that the thought of death was the only thing which at this time gave her relief. She said: "Sometimes it seems to me that my patience is exhausted and that I am on the point of giving up everything and of abandoning myself to perdition." For the last eight or nine years of her life, her temptations, instead of diminishing, became more terrible, so that whether she was praying or working, her interior martyrdom was such as to excite compassion in everyone who was intimate with her. It seemed to her sometimes that God drove her from Him, so that to relieve herself, she turned her thoughts away from God. But not finding the relief she sought, she turned again to the contemplation of God, even though He seemed angry with her. In meditations, in Communions and in other devout exercises, she experienced nothing but weariness and anguish. She seemed to herself to be like a sick person overwhelmed with diseases, incapable of turning herself to another side; dumb, so as not to be able to explain her sufferings; and blind, so that she could see no way of escaping from the depths of her misery. She seemed to have lost divine love, and Hope, and Faith; for the rest, she kept her eyes fixed upon God, reposing in the arms of the Divine Will. In a word, St. Francis de Sales used to say of her that her blessed soul was like a deaf musician, who sang most admirably, but had no pleasure in his voice, because he could not hear it. The soul, therefore, which finds itself tried with dryness must not lose courage, however much it may feel overwhelmed by darkness, but must trust in the blood of Jesus Christ and resign itself to the Divine Will and say:

"O Jesus, my Hope, and the only Love of my soul, I deserve not consolations; give them to those who have always loved Thee; I have deserved Hell and to be there forever, abandoned by Thee without hope of ever being able to love Thee. But no, my Saviour, I accept every suffering; chastise me as much as Thou wilt, but deprive me not of the power of loving Thee. Take from me everything, but not Thyself. Miserable as I am, I love Thee more than myself, and I give myself wholly to Thee; I resolve to live no more for myself. Give me strength to be faithful to Thee.

"O holy Virgin, Hope of Sinners, I place my confidence in thy intercession; make me love my God, for He has created and has redeemed me."

Reflection 40

On a Life of Retirement

SOULS that love God find their paradise in a retired life in which they are removed from intercourse with men. No, to converse with God, withdrawing one's self from creatures, does not bring bitterness or weariness. "His conversation hath no bitterness, nor His company any tediousness, but joy and gladness." (Cf. *Wisdom* 8:16).

Worldly people, with good reason, flee from solitude, because in solitude, where they are not occupied with diversions or worldly affairs, the remorse of conscience makes itself felt more in their hearts; and therefore such persons seek to relieve themselves, or at least to distract their thoughts, by conversing with men; but the more they study to relieve themselves among men and among worldly affairs, the more they meet with thorns and bitter disappointments.

To the lovers of God this does not happen, because in retirement they find a Sweet Companion who consoles them and makes them glad, more than the company of all their friends or relations, or of the highest personages of the earth. St. Bernard used to say: "I am never less alone than when alone, never less alone than when far from men, for then I find God, who speaks to me, and then I see myself, on the other hand, more attentive to His voice and more disposed to unite myself to Him." Our Blessed Saviour desired that His disciples, notwithstanding that He had destined them to propagate the Faith by journeying throughout the whole world, should from time to time cease their labors and retire into solitude, to treat with God alone. We know, moreover, that Jesus Christ, even at the time when He was living on earth, was accustomed to send them into different parts of Judea, that they might convert sinners; but after their labors, He did not fail to invite them to retire to some solitary place, saying to them: "Come apart into a desert place, and rest a little. For there were many coming and going, and they had not so much as time to eat." (*Matthew* 6:31).

If Our Lord said even to the Apostles, "rest a little," it is therefore necessary for all apostolic laborers to retire from time to time into solitude to preserve their spirit of recollection and union with God and to obtain strength to labor afterwards with greater vigor for the salvation of souls.

He that labors for his neighbor with but little zeal and with little love for God, having some end in view dictated by self-love, of seeking to gain honor or wealth, does little for gaining souls. Therefore, Our Lord says to His laborers: "Rest a little." Certainly Jesus Christ did not mean by this expression that the Apostles were to go to sleep, but that they should repose in holding communion with God, in praying to Him for the graces necessary for living well, and thus should gain strength to employ themselves afterwards for the salvation of souls. Otherwise, without this repose with God in prayer, there is an absence of the vigor necessary to attend well to one's own progress and to the profit of others.

St. Lawrence Justinian, speaking of retirement, wisely remarks that it is to be always loved, but not always enjoyed: meaning to say that they who are called by God to labor for the conversion of sinners must not remain always in solitude, shut up in a cell, for they would be neglecting their divine vocation, to obey which, when God calls them, they must leave their retirement. Yet they should never cease to love and to sigh for solitude, in which God allows Himself to be more easily found.

O my Jesus, I have loved retirement little, because I have loved Thee little. I have gone seeking pleasures and relaxations from creatures, who have made me lose Thee, the Infinite Good. Alas, that for so many years I have kept my heart dissipated, thinking only of the goods of earth, and forgetting Thee! Oh take Thou for Thyself this heart of mine, since Thou hast purchased it with Thy blood! Inflame it with Thy love and make it entirely Thine own.

O Mary, Queen of Heaven, thou canst obtain for me this grace; from thee I hope for it.

Reflection 41

On Detachment from Creatures

IN ORDER to attain to loving God with all our hearts, we must detach ourselves from everything which is not God, or does not tend toward God. He wills to be alone in the possession of our hearts; He admits no companions there, and with reason, because He is our only Lord, who has given us everything. Yet more, He is our only Lover, who loves us, not for His own interest, but solely out of His Goodness; and because He loves us exceedingly, He demands that we should love Him with all our hearts: "Thou shalt love the Lord thy God with thy whole heart." (*Matthew* 22:37).

To love God with our whole heart implies two things: the first is to banish every affection which is not for God, or according to the will of God. "If I knew," said St. Francis de Sales, "that there was one fiber in my heart which did not belong to God, I would instantly tear it out." The second is prayer, by which divine love is introduced into the heart. But if the heart does not empty itself of all that is of the earth, love cannot enter, for it finds no room for itself. On the contrary, a heart detached from all creatures becomes quickly inflamed and increases in divine love at every breath of grace.

"Pure love," says the holy Bishop of Geneva, "consumes everything which is not God, in order to change it into itself, because everything which is done for God, is love of God." Oh how full of goodness and liberality is God to the soul which seeks nothing but Him and His Will! "The Lord is good . . . to the soul that seeketh Him." (*Lamentations* 3:25). Happy is he who, still living in the world, can say with truth, as did St. Francis: "My God and my all!" And thus he can hold in contempt all the vanities of the world. "I have despised the kingdom of the world and all worldly honor for the love of Jesus Christ, my Lord."

When, therefore, creatures would enter into our heart and take a share of that love, which we owe entirely to God, we must immediately dismiss them, shutting the door against them and saying: "Begone; go to those who desire you; my heart I have given wholly to Jesus Christ; there is no room for you." And besides this resolution to desire nothing but God, we likewise must hate that which the world loves and love that which the world hates.

Above all, to attain to perfect love, we must deny ourselves, embracing that which is distasteful to self-love and rejecting that which self-love demands. A certain thing is pleasant to us; for that very reason we must refuse it. A certain medicine is disagreeable, because it is bitter; we must take it, just because it is bitter. We do not like to oblige a certain person who has been ungrateful to us; we must by all means do him good, precisely because he has been ungrateful.

St. Francis de Sales says, moreover, that we must love even virtues with detachment; for example, we ought to love meditation and retirement; but when they are forbidden to us through the calls of obedience or of charity, we must leave both the one and the other without being disquieted. And thus it is necessary to embrace with equanimity everything which happens to us through the Will of God. Happy is he who wishes, or does not wish for, whatever happens to him, because God wills or does not will it, without inclining to either side. And therefore, we must beg of God to enable us to find peace in everything which He appoints us.

Let us listen to the words of Cardinal Petrucci, who in a few lines describes well the folly of the lovers of the world and the happiness of the lovers of God:

> "What is this fickle world
>   So false and vain?
> A scene of blasted hopes,
>   Remorse and pain.
> Its sweetest charms, its feasts,
>   Its gilded toys
> Bring tortures, though they seemed
>   Nought else but joys.
> Then bravely follow Christ,
>   The cross endure:
> It seems to torture, yet
>   Gives joys most pure."

It is certain that no one lives more happily in the world, than he who despises the things of the world and lives in continual uniformity with the Will of God. Therefore, it is useful frequently during the day, at least at prayer and Communion, to renew at the foot of the crucifix the total renouncement of ourselves and of all we have, saying:

"O my Jesus, I desire to think no more of myself; I give myself wholly to Thee; do with me what Thou pleasest. I see that everything that the world offers me is vanity and deceit. From this day, I resolve to seek nothing but Thee and Thy good pleasure; help me to be faithful to Thee.

"Most Holy Virgin Mary, pray to Jesus for me."

Reflection 42

Precious Is the
Death of the Saints

"**P**RECIOUS in the sight of the Lord is the death of His Saints." (*Psalms* 115:15). Why is the death of the Saints called precious? "Because," replies St. Bernard, "it is so rich in blessings that it deserves to be purchased at any price."

Some persons attached to this world would wish that there was no such thing as death; but St. Augustine says: "What is it to live long upon this earth except to remain long in suffering?" "The miseries and sorrows which constantly afflict us in this present life are so great," says St. Ambrose, "that death seems rather a relief than a punishment."

Death terrifies sinners because they know that from the first death, if they die in sin, they will pass to the second death, which is eternal; but it does not terrify the good, who, trusting in the merits of Jesus Christ, have sufficient signs to give them a moral assurance that they are in the grace of God. Wherefore, those words, "Depart, Christian soul, from this world," which are so terrible to those who die against their will, do not afflict the Saints, who have preserved their hearts free from worldly love and with a true affection were always repeating: "My God and my all."

To these, death is not a torment, but a rest from the

anguish they have suffered in struggling with temptations and in quieting their scruples and their fear of offending God, so that what St. John writes of them is fulfilled: "Blessed are the dead who die in the Lord! From henceforth now, saith the Spirit, that they may rest from their labors." (*Apocalypse* 14:13). He that dies loving God is not disturbed by the pains which death brings with it; but rather, he is glad of them, that he may offer them to God as the last remnants of his life. Oh what peace is experienced by him who dies when he has abandoned himself into the arms of Jesus Christ, who chose for Himself a death of bitterness and desolation, that He might obtain for us a death of sweetness and resignation!

O my Jesus, Thou art my judge, but Thou art also my Redeemer, who hast died to save me. From the time of my first sin, I deserved to be condemned to Hell, but in Thy mercy Thou hast given me a deep sorrow for my sins; wherefore, I confidently hope that now Thou hast pardoned me. I did not deserve to love Thee anymore, but Thou by Thy benefits hast drawn me to Thy love. If it is Thy will that death should come to me in this sickness, I willingly accept it. I well see that I do not deserve to enter Paradise at once; I go contented to Purgatory, to suffer as long as it pleases Thee. There my greatest pain will be to remain far from Thee, sighing to come and see Thee and love Thee face to face. Therefore, O my beloved Saviour, have pity on me.

And what else is this present life but a state of perpetual danger of losing God? "We walk amidst snares," says St. Ambrose; amidst the snares and deceits of enemies who seek to make us lose the divine grace. Therefore, St. Teresa, every time that the clock struck, gave thanks to God that another hour of struggle and peril had passed without sin; and therefore also, she was so rejoiced at the tidings that her death was at hand, considering that her conflicts were over and the time was near for her to depart and behold her God.

In this present life we cannot live without defects. This is the motive which makes souls that love God even desire death. It was this thought which, at the time of death, rejoiced Father Vincent Carafa when he said: "Now that I finish my life, I cease to offend God." A certain virtuous man gave directions to his attendants that, at the time of his death, they should often repeat to him these words: "Comfort thyself, because the time is near when thou wilt no more offend God."

And what else is this body to us but a prison in which the soul is confined, so that it cannot depart to unite itself with God? On this account, St. Francis, inflamed with love at the hour of his death, cried out with the prophet: "Bring my soul out of prison." (*Psalms* 141:8). O Lord, deliver me from this prison which prevents me from seeing Thee. O amiable death, who can fear thee and not desire thee, since thou art the end of labor and the beginning of eternal life! St. Pionius the Martyr, standing by the scaffold, showed himself so full of joy that the people who stood by wondered at his delight and asked him how he could be so happy when he was just about to die. "You are mistaken," said he, "you are mistaken; I am not hastening to death, but to life."

O most sweet Jesus, I thank Thee for not having made me die when I was under Thy wrath and for having won my heart by so many loving artifices which Thou hast employed. When I think of the displeasure I have often given Thee, I should wish to die of grief. This my soul, which once was lost, I now commit wholly into Thy hands. "Into Thy hands I commend my spirit." (*Luke* 23:46). Remember, O Lord, that Thou hast

redeemed it with Thy death. "Thou hast redeemed me,
O Lord, the God of truth." (*Psalms* 30:6). I love Thee,
O Infinite Goodness, and I desire to depart quickly
from this life, that I may come and love Thee with a
more perfect love in Heaven. Meanwhile, as long as I
shall live on this earth, make me know always better
my obligation to love Thee. O my God, receive me; I
give myself wholly to Thee, and I put my trust in Thee
through the merits of Jesus Christ.

I trust also in thy intercession, O Mary, my hope.

Reflection 43

On Lukewarmness

THERE are two kinds of lukewarmness: one which can be avoided, and the other which cannot be avoided. Unavoidable tepidity is that which in the present life is endured even by fervent souls because, through natural weakness, they cannot avoid falling from time to time into some slight fault, but without full consent. From such defects, no one, because of the corruption of our nature through Original Sin, is free, without a most special grace, which was granted to no one but the Mother of God. God Himself permits these imperfections in His Saints in order to keep them humble. Often they find themselves without fervor, full of weariness and disgust in their devout exercises; and at such times of dryness they are more apt to fall into many defects, at least without deliberation. For the rest, let not those who find themselves in this condition leave off their usual devotions, nor lose courage, nor believe that they have fallen into lukewarmness, for this is not lukewarmness. Let them go on with their accustomed exercises, let them detest their defects, let them often renew their resolution of giving themselves wholly to God, and let them have confidence in Him, for He will console them. There is true and deplorable lukewarmness when the soul falls into venial sins which are quite voluntary and grieves but little for them and takes even less care to avoid them, saying that they are trifles of no consequence. What! Is it nothing to displease God? St. Teresa used to say to her nuns: "My daughters, may God preserve you from willful sins, however small."

Some people say: "But such sins do not deprive us of the grace of God." He who says this is in great danger of seeing himself one day deprived of divine grace and in a state of mortal sin. St. Gregory writes that whoever falls into deliberate venial sins habitually, without feeling pain at it and without thinking of correcting himself, does not remain where he is, but will go on and fall down a precipice. [i.e., into mortal sin]. "The soul never stays on the spot where it falls." Mortal diseases do not always spring from serious disorders, but often from many slight disorders of long continuance; and thus the fall of certain souls into a state of sin is often to be attributed to the repetition of venial sins, which make the soul so weak, that when attacked by any violent temptation, it has no strength to resist and therefore falls.

"He that contemneth [shows contempt for] small things shall fall by little and little." (*Ecclesiasticus* 19:1). He that makes no account of trifling falls, will one day find himself down a precipice [i.e., in mortal sin]. Our Lord said: "Because thou art lukewarm, I will begin to vomit thee out of My mouth." (*Apocalypse* 3:16). This signifies that the soul will be abandoned by God, or at least deprived of those special divine aids which are necessary to preserve us in the state of grace. Let us understand well this point: The Council of Trent condemns those who say that we can persevere in grace without a special help from God: "If any one shall say that a man who is justified . . . can persevere in the justice he has received without the special help of God, . . . let him be anathema." (Council of Trent, Session 6, Canon 22). Therefore, we cannot persevere in grace without a special extraordinary help from God; but this special help God will justly refuse to one who makes no account of committing many venial sins with his eyes open. Is God bound to give this special help to one who does not abstain from willfully causing Him continual displeasure? "He who soweth sparingly, shall also reap sparingly." (*2 Corinthians* 9:6). If we are niggardly with God, how can we hope that God will be generous towards us?

Miserable is that soul which makes peace with sins, even when venial! He will go from bad to worse; for his passions, ever gaining ground upon him, will easily blind him; and when a man is blind, it is easy for him to find himself fallen down a precipice [into mortal sin] when least he expects it. Let us fear to fall into voluntary tepidity, for it is like hectic fever [consumption, i.e., tuberculosis], which does not cause much alarm, but is so malignant that with great difficulty is anyone cured of it.

For the rest, though it is very difficult for a lukewarm person to amend, yet there are remedies, if only he is resolved to amend. The remedies are: 1) a resolution to escape at all costs from this miserable state; 2) to remove the occasion of falling, without which there is no hope of amendment; and 3) frequently to recommend himself to God with fervent prayer, that He would give him strength to come out of this deplorable condition and not to cease praying until he finds himself delivered from it.

O Lord, have mercy on me. I see that I deserve to be cast forth by Thee for so many defects with which I serve Thee. Miserable that I am, it is for this reason I find myself without love, without confidence and without good desires. O my Jesus, abandon me not;

stretch forth Thy powerful hand and draw me out of this depth of lukewarmness in which I see myself fallen. Grant this through the merits of Thy Passion, in which I place my confidence.

O holy Virgin, pray to Jesus for me.

Reflection 44

On Purity of Intention

PURITY of intention consists in performing everything we do solely to please God. Jesus Christ has said that according to the intention, whether it be good or evil, such before God is the action performed. "If thy eye be evil, thy whole body shall be darksome." (*Matthew* 6:23). The single eye signifies a pure intention of pleasing God; the dark and evil eye signifies an intention which is not pure, as when our actions are done out of vanity or to please ourselves.

Can any action be more noble than to give one's life for the Faith? And yet St. Paul says, that he who dies from any motive but to please God gains nothing by his martyrdom.

If, then, even martyrdom profits nothing, unless it be endured for God, of what value will be all the preaching, all the labors of apostolic men, and also all the austerities of penitents, if they are done to obtain the praise of men or to gratify one's inclination?

The prophet Aggæus says that works, although holy in themselves, if not done for God, are put into bags full of holes—which means that they are all lost directly and that nothing remains of them. On the contrary, every action done with an intention of pleasing God, of however little value in itself, is worth more than many works done without a pure intention.

We read in St. Mark that the poor widow cast into the chest for alms in the Temple only two mites, but yet of her our Saviour said: "This poor widow hath cast in more than all." (*Mark* 12:43). St. Cyprian remarks on this that she put in more than all the others because she gave those two little pieces of money with the pure intention of pleasing God.

One of the best signs by which to know if a person acts with a right intention is that, if the work have not the effect desired, he will not be at all disturbed. Another good sign is that, when he has performed any work and afterwards is spoken ill of for it, or is repaid with ingratitude, he nevertheless remains contented and tranquil. For the rest, should he happen to be praised for it, he ought not to disquiet himself with the fear of vainglory; but should the thought present itself, let him despise it and say with St. Bernard: "I did not begin it for thee, nor because of thee will I leave it."

To act with an intention of acquiring more glory in Heaven is good, but the most perfect intention is to please God. Let us be persuaded that the more we divest ourselves of our own interests, so much the more will Our Lord increase our joy in Paradise. Blessed is he who labors only to give glory to God and to follow His holy will! Let us imitate the love of the Blessed who, in loving God, seek only to please Him. St. Chrysostom says: "If thou hast the honor of doing anything that pleases God, how canst thou ask any other reward?"

This is that single eye which pierces the heart of God with love toward us; as He said to the sacred Spouse: "Thou hast wounded My heart, My sister, My spouse; thou hast wounded My heart with one of thy eyes." (*Canticle of Canticles* 4:9). This one eye signifies the one end that holy souls have in all their actions, that of pleasing God. And this was the counsel that the Apostle gave to his disciples: "Therefore, whether you eat or drink, or whatsoever else you do, do all to the glory of God." (*1 Corinthians* 10:31). The venerable Beatrice of the Incarnation, the first daughter of St. Teresa, said: "No sufficient price could be paid for anything, however small, which is done for God." And with reason did she say this, for all works done for God are acts of divine love. Purity of intention makes the lowest actions become precious, such as eating, working, or even taking recreation, when all is done from obedience, and to please God.

We must, then, from the very morning direct to God all the actions of the day; and it is very profitable to renew this intention at the beginning of every action, at least of the most important, such as meditation, Communion, and spiritual reading; pausing a little at the beginning of these, like that holy hermit who, before beginning anything he had to do, lifted his eyes to Heaven and remained still; and when he was asked what he was then doing, he replied: "I am making sure of my aim."

And I, O my Jesus, when shall I begin to love Thee truly? Alas, for me! If I seek among my works, even those that are good, for one action done only to please Thee, my Saviour, I do not find it. Ah then, have pity on me, and suffer me not to serve Thee so ill, even till my death! Grant me Thy help, that what remains to me of life I may spend only in serving and loving Thee. Make me overcome all, that I may please Thee and do everything only to give Thee pleasure. Through the merits of Thy Passion I ask it.

O my great Advocate, Mary, obtain for me this grace by thy prayers.

Reflection 45

Sighs for our Heavenly Home

HAPPY is he who is saved and who, leaving this place of exile, enters into the heavenly Jerusalem, to enjoy that perfect day which shall be always day and always joyful, free from all cares and from all fear of ever losing that immense happiness.

The patriarch Jacob said: "The days of my pilgrimage are a hundred and thirty years, few and evil." (*Genesis* 47:9). The same may be said by us miserable pilgrims, while we remain on this earth, enduring the labors of our exile, distressed by temptations, harassed by passions, and afflicted by miseries and still more by the dangers to our eternal salvation. Seeing all this, we should reflect that this is not our home, but a land of exile where God detains us, in order that we may, by suffering, merit to enter one day into the happy country of Heaven.

And therefore, living detached from this earth, we ought always to sigh for Paradise saying: "When shall it be, O Lord, that I shall be delivered from so many anxieties and think of nothing but of loving Thee and praising Thee? When shall it be that Thou wilt be all to me in all things, as the Apostle writes: 'That God may be all in all?' (*1 Corinthians* 15:28). When shall

I enjoy that unchanging peace, free from all affliction and from all danger of being lost? When, O my God, shall I find myself swallowed up in Thee and behold Thine infinite beauty, face to face and without veil? When, in a word, O my Creator, shall I attain to the possession of Thee in such a manner that I may say: 'My God, I cannot lose Thee anymore?'"

Meanwhile, O my Saviour, while Thou seest me an exile and afflicted in this land of enemies, where I have to be fighting in ceaseless internal wars, help me by Thy grace and console me in this so sorrowful a pilgrimage. Whatever the world may offer me, I already know that nothing in it can give me peace and satisfy me; but yet I fear lest, if I have not help from Thee, the pleasures of the world and my evil inclinations may draw me down some precipice [of committing mortal sin].

Seeing myself an exile in this valley of tears, I would wish at least to think of Thee continually, O my God, and rejoice in that infinite happiness which Thou enjoyest; but the evil desires of the senses often cry out within me and disturb me. I would wish to keep my affections ever occupied in loving Thee and thanking Thee, but the flesh entices me to enjoy sensual delights; hence, I am constrained to exclaim with St. Paul: "Unhappy man that I am, who shall deliver me from the body of this death?" (*Romans* 7:24). Miserable man that I am, in continual combat, not only with external enemies, but with myself, so that I am weighted down and a trouble to myself! "I am become burdensome to myself," said holy Job. (*Job* 7:20).

Who, then, will deliver me from the body of this death, that is, from the danger of falling into sin, from that peril, the fear only of which is to me a continual death, which torments me and will not cease to torment me all my life through? "O God, be not Thou far from me; O my God, make haste to my help." (*Psalms* 70:12).

My God, go not far from me, because if Thou goest from me, I fear I shall displease Thee. Rather, draw nearer to me with Thy powerful help; that is, succor me continually, that I may be able to resist the attacks of my enemies. The Royal Prophet tells me that Thou art near, that is, that Thou dost give holy patience to all who are sorrowful of heart and are in interior affliction. "The Lord is nigh unto them that are of a contrite heart." (*Psalms* 33:19). Remain very near me, then, my beloved Saviour, and give me that patience that I need to overcome the continual attacks by which I am tormented. How often, when I apply myself to prayer, do not troublesome thoughts draw me away and distract me with a thousand follies! Do Thou give me strength to drive them from me, when occupied with Thee, and crucify all the evil inclinations that hinder me from uniting myself with Thee. And take from me, I pray Thee, the great repugnance that I feel to embrace with resignation anything that is not agreeable to my self-love.

O house of my God, prepared for those that love Thee, to Thee I sigh from this land of misery. "I have gone astray, like a sheep that is lost; seek Thy servant." (*Psalms* 118:176). O beloved Shepherd of my soul, who didst descend from Heaven to seek and to save the lost sheep, behold, I am one who, turning my back on Thee, am miserably lost. Seek Thy servant, seek me, O Lord; abandon me not as I deserve; seek me and save me; take me and hold me tight upon Thy shoulders, that I may not leave Thee again.

But, even while I am longing for Paradise, my enemy is terrifying me with the remembrance of my sins; but the sight of Thee, my crucified Jesus, consoles me and gives me courage to hope that one day I shall come to love Thee and behold Thee unveiled in Thy blessed Kingdom.

Queen of Heaven, continue to be my advocate. Through the blood of Jesus Christ and through thy intercession, I have a firm hope of being saved.

St. Alphonsus Liguori
1696-1787
Bishop and Doctor
of the Church

Born in 1696 to a noble Italian family near Naples, St. Alphonsus Liguori eventually received two law degrees at age 16. After practicing law for a few years he decided to leave the world; he was ordained a priest in 1726.

St. Alphonsus is known as the "Prince of Moral Theologians." His classic work, *Moral Theology*, gave sound teaching for moral theologians and confessors, avoiding both Jansenism and laxity. During the years he spent as a missionary in the Kingdom of Naples (1726-1752), his confessional line was crowded with penitents. Later, as Bishop of Saint Agatha, St. Alphonsus instructed his priests to practice simplicity in the pulpit and charity in the confessional.

St. Alphonsus Liguori founded the Redemptorist Order. Its special work is to give parish missions, rejuvenating faith and fervor by several days of special days of sermons and the hearing of Confessions. Due to some unfortunate circumstances, there was a split existing in the Redemptorist Order at the time of St. Alphonsus' death. Other sufferings that he endured were an illness which left him with a permanently bent neck—which can be seen in some portraits, and interior trials, including scruples, that came to him in his old age. Yet despite trials, St. Alphonsus always acted with purity of intention, that is, for God alone, without consideration of self-will. He died in 1787 at the age of 90.

St. Alphonsus wrote over 100 books and shorter works. Among the most famous are *The Glories of Mary, The True Spouse of Jesus Christ, The Way of Salva-*

tion, The Great Means of Salvation and Perfection, An Exposition and Defence of All the Points of Faith discussed and defined by the Sacred Council of Trent along with a Refutation of the Errors of the Pretended Reformers, and *Visits to the Blessed Sacrament and the Blessed Virgin Mary.* Pope Pius IX declared St. Alphonsus Liguori a Doctor of the Church, thus giving an authoritative stamp of approval to the teachings of the saintly bishop and founder.